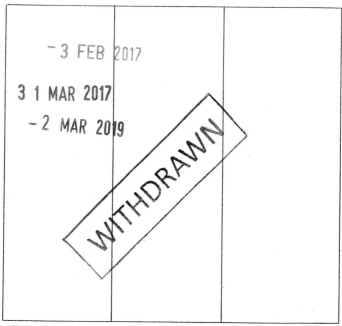

Paranormal PERTHSHIRE

Geoff Holder

The History Press

In memory of my grandparents

Frontispiece: The Maggie Wall Monument near Dunning sometime between 1900 and 1910. (*A.K. Bell Library, Local Studies*)

First published 2011

The History Press
The Mill, Brimscombe Port
Stroud, Gloucestershire, GL5 2QG
www.thehistorypress.co.uk

© Geoff Holder, 2011

The right of Geoff Holder to be identified as the Author
of this work has been asserted in accordance with the
Copyrights, Designs and Patents Act 1988.

British Library Cataloguing in Publication Data.
A catalogue record for this book is available from the British Library.

ISBN 978 0 7524 5421 4

Typesetting and origination by The History Press
Printed in Great Britain
Manufacturing managed by Jellyfish Print Solutions Ltd

CONTENTS

ACKNOWLEDGEMENTS

My thanks go out to: Thomas Brown; David Connolly; David Cowan; Simon Cowan of the Dunning Historical Society; David Doig; Lynn Dukes of the *Strathearn Herald*; Ségolène Dupuy, *comme toujours*; Robbie Duncan; Jeannie Fox; Scott Fraser; Alex Graeme; Heather McDonald; James and Wilma Marshall; Lord and Lady Moncreiff; Professor David M. Munro and the staff of the Kinross-shire Historical Society; John Murray, the St Fillans correspondent of *The Villagers* newsletter; Keith Ringland, www.ringlandlifeimages.co.uk; James Sheriff; T & M Stonemasons; John and Bronwen Wheatley; Elma Wood; and the many people who contacted me to share their stories, but who preferred to remain anonymous.

Further praise is heaped on the indefatigable staff of the A.K. Bell Library Local Studies Department, Perth, and the equally committed staff of the National Archives of Scotland in Edinburgh.

I would like to particularly express my appreciation to the Graeme family for sharing with me their news clippings, family history, and photographs.

Except where indicated, all maps are reproduced courtesy of the A.K. Library Local Studies Department, Perth.

INTRODUCTION

The end of 2006 saw the publication of my first book, *The Guide to Mysterious Perthshire*. Here, sixteen volumes later, I return to the county with *Paranormal Perthshire*. This is a very different book. Rather than take a village-by-village, glen-by-glen geographical approach as in the earlier work, here we find tales of the supernatural and strange arranged in thematic chapters. So within the following pages you can, for example, find comprehensive surveys of sightings of two persistent modern mysteries – UFOs and big cats (and I consider it much more likely that you are likely to come across a puma or panther than a visitor from Zeta Reticuli).

Elsewhere we delve into the past, with a re-assessment of the alleged 'haunting' at Ballechin House in Strathtay, an affair that scandalised upper-class Victorian readers of *The Times* and cast a shadow over psychical research. Then there are a series of personal experiences of the paranormal, as related by people from up and down Perth and Kinross. These include encounters with ghosts, spiritual beings, invisible entities, dark forces and angelic visitants, and powerful examples of the mysterious bonds that may link us to the natural world.

The Maggie Wall Monument at Dunning, the subject of Chapter Four. *(Photo by Geoff Holder)*

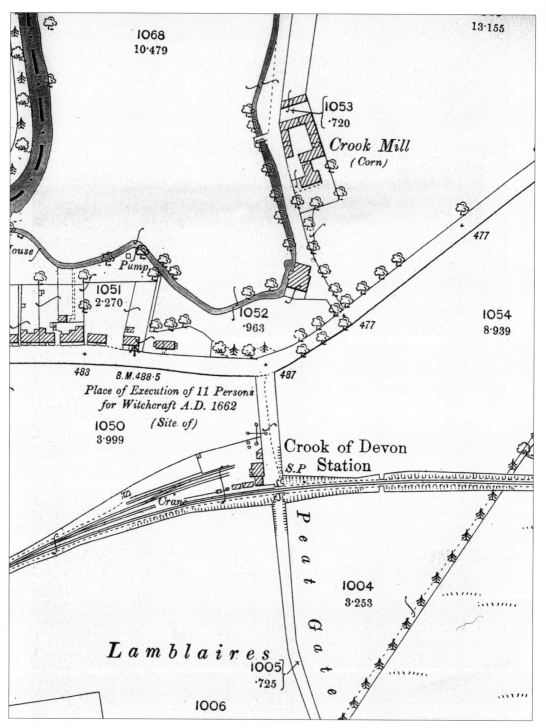

The place of execution at Crook of Devon, shown on the first edition of the Ordnance Survey map in the 1860s. *(Courtesy A.K. Bell Library, Local Studies)*

Above: The site at Lamblaires, Crook of Devon, where 11 men and women were executed for witchcraft in 1662. *(Photo by Geoff Holder)*

Right: The sign for the Witches Maze near Tullibole Castle, Crook of Devon. *(Photo by Geoff Holder)*

Below: Some of the 2000 beech trees planted by Lord Moncreiff for the Witches Maze. *(Photo by Geoff Holder)*

The Witches Maze

When finished this maze will be a memorial to the 11 innocent persons who met their doom at Crook of Devon after 5 trials in 1662
In the maze will be 11 carved stones including a 3ft hexagonal pillar in the centre.
The maze was planted in a circular 100ft diameter area that may have been a secret garden or a horse training ring.

Do not enter after dark!!

Mysterious Perthshire touched on two of Perthshire's enduring conundrums, the Maggie Wall Witch Monument at Dunning, and the story of Kate McNiven, the Witch of Monzie – both 'famous' witches who may not have existed. Here both are reconsidered in hugely expanded detail, including material never before published. It is my modest belief that I have solved at least part of the Maggie Wall mystery (and that this solution may not be to the taste of those who are emotionally committed to her legend). As for Kate McNiven – well, her weird tales continue to perplex and bamboozle, but have I succeeded in penetrating through the miasma? You can make your judgment.

The witchcraft trials remain a hot topic in Perth and Kinross. In 1662 – one of the worst years in the witchcraft frenzy – thirteen people were put on trial in Crook of Devon. Agnes Pittendreich was temporarily released on account of her pregnancy; seventy-nine-year-old Margaret Hogginn probably died of old age or neglect shortly after the trial. The other eleven were taken to Lamblaires, just south of the present Village Institute, strangled by the hangman and burnt to ashes. The proceedings had seen an unedifying lust for torture and persecution headed by a self-appointed cabal of local busybodies led by William Halliday, the laird of Tullibole Castle. The present owner of Tullibole, Lord Moncreiff, has decided to make amends, and in 2003 planted a 'Witch Maze' of 2000 beech trees as a memorial to the murdered eleven. As of 2011 there is a pillar at the centre of the maze, carved with the names of those executed, and further stones inscribed with 'good words' embracing tolerance and wisdom contrasted with 'bad words' indicating the viciousness and ignorance expressed at the witch trials. This extraordinary site has free public access from Gelvan Road, the minor road linking the A977 and B9097 east of Crook of Devon (Tullibole Castle itself is private).

Perthshire is still a place where supernatural belief and the more mundane aspects of everyday life are intertwined. In the autumn of 2005 a housing development in the village of St Fillans was allegedly delayed because local people were incensed that it would destroy a 'fairy stone'. Soon it was not just the local press, but also *The Times* and other national papers that splashed the story, and then the BBC, the Canadian Broadcasting Co. and other television channels turned up. Everyone loved the 'fairy tale'.

The reality was not quite so simple, as I found when I tried to dig deeper into the story. The rock was a large glacial erratic sitting in a field where people walked their dogs; it did not feature in local folklore or in any of the books on Strathearn history, archaeology or legend, and was not that different from other stones in the area. There was no existing tradition. When the story broke there were vague notions bruited about that plague victims had been buried there, or that it was some kind of chieftainship stone, or it was on a ley-line – but no-one could point to a belief that fairies lived under the stone. The general feeling was what one paper called 'Feng MacShui' – a notion that prominent features in the landscape should remain where they are.

Having spoken to several of the people involved, I get the sense that the story grew out of some very specific circumstances. Many residents in the village were opposed to the housing development. Because of the local feeling, there is a degree of 'he said, she said' in the recall of the events. One suggestion is that the story of the fairy stone was invented to help the opposition to the development, and that it simply got out of control. Another version is that one of the residents in the neighbouring properties mentioned the 'spirits' under the stone (resulting from the alleged plague burials) and that the developer's PR agent transmuted this into 'fairies'; once a press release was sent out, the world's media descended.

Above: The 'Fairy Stone' at St Fillans.
(Photo by Geoff Holder)

Right: Some of the many coin offerings
pushed into the crevices of the Fairy Stone.
(Photo by Geoff Holder)

The Crocodile Stone, St Fillans. *(Photo by Geoff Holder)*

Yet a third version has a resident dramatically running out to prevent a bulldozer removing the stone, shouting that it would disturb the fairies. Whatever the exact circumstances, the stone was allowed to remain in its initial location.

Irrespective of how it started, once the 'fairy stone' story was up and running, it was impossible to stop. At one point Crieff-based 'earth energies' enthusiast David Cowan was called in to give his opinion. He claimed to have found two tiny and very shallow cupmarks on the top of the stone (although I have failed to locate these elusive features). Cupmarks are forms of prehistoric rock art, enigmatic bowl-shaped depressions whose purpose and meaning are still much debated. David told me how he placed sweets in the marks to make them more obvious. A journalist asked him what he was doing, and he jokingly replied he was leaving an offering for the fairies. The reporter added two £1 coins, as did the developer. A few days later David returned to take photographs, and found the coins and sweets still there – but someone had added some peanuts.

Over the following months and years many more items were left at the stone, with families making specific trips out to St Fillans so their children could see it. Many of the kids wrote to the developers thanking them for saving the fairy stone. These days, every nook and cranny on the stone is crammed with coins. What might have begun as an oppositional tactic or a PR gambit has now become fully established in the fairy folklore of Scotland.

Meanwhile, a mile from the fairy stone, a rock outcrop has for many years been painted in the form of a monster or crocodile. Why? Just because.

In conclusion, there is no conclusion. Things go on as they always have, getting weirder all the time.

Robert Anton Wilson, Introduction to *Principia Discordia*

ONE

BIG CATS

'I thought I saw a pussy cat!'

For decades there have been reports that the British countryside is home to a population of exotic big cats. Judging by the descriptions, the most common candidates seem to be: tawny-coloured pumas (also known as cougars, and native to the Americas, Latin name *Puma concolor*); the similarly-coloured Eurasian lynx (*Felis lynx*), which has distinctive tufted ears and was native to Britain until the early Middle Ages; and the black panther, which originates from Asia and Africa. Black panthers (*Panthera pardus*) are actually leopards that possess a genetic mutation called melanism, which produces black fur rather than the typical leopard's spots. Melanistic leopards are very rare in the wild, yet according to the reports they are probably the most commonly-sighted creatures in these isles, a situation that makes sceptics dismiss the entire notion of big cats in Britain as simply impossible.

This extremely sceptical position – that there are no 'alien big cats' roaming our land at all – is one of three basic responses to the 'big cat' question. From this first perspective, the multiple sightings can be put down to simple misidentification. Most people are not intimately familiar with the appearance and behaviour of large cat species, and so a brief glimpse of a felid can be mistakenly interpreted as an exotic creature, when the animal is actually a more ordinary critter.

A black panther. *(The Imperial Dictionary, 1859)*

A leopard, *Panthera pardus*. *(The Imperial Dictionary, 1859)*

Typically the usual suspects for these home-grown cats are threefold: domestic cats that have turned feral; the reclusive and now-endangered native Scottish wildcat (*Felis silvestris grampia*); and the Kellas cat, a hybrid between Scottish wildcats and feral domestic moggies. Other candidates for 'big cat' sightings include large dogs (misidentified in poor lighting conditions), foxes, and unusual breeds of domestic cat. Certainly witnesses can often be mistaken – for example, in 2010 several people in Dundee reported seeing a dangerous 'big cat', which turned out to simply be a large example of a pedigree breed called a Maine Coon Cat.

The notion that the whole 'big cat' idea has no base in reality is often a position offered by some authorities such as police wildlife officers, natural heritage workers and conservation consultants; there is the distinct possibility that such individuals fear for their professional reputations if they start acknowledging 'fringe' ideas such as big cats. (A similar professional reluctance prevents many scientists from engaging with other mysteries such as loch monsters, Psi powers and UFOs – they fear being tarred with the taint of weirdness. But it's only rigorous scientific analysis that will detach these mysteries from the realm of mystical obscurity, conspiracy theories and occult posturing.) On the other hand, the Wildlife Liaison Officer from Dorset constabulary contends that several big cats are definitely at large in the West Country of England, while a live puma was trapped in Inverness-shire in 1980, and one of the smallest exotic felines, the leopard cat (*Felis bengalensis*) was shot near Jedburgh in 1988, with the body of a second found in Berwickshire in 1990.

An entirely different perspective comes from the notion that the big cats are not real flesh-and-blood animals at all. The suggestion here is that they are members of some kind of 'phantom menagerie', supernatural tourists from another realm who visit our world for short times, then flit back to their own dimension. This idea was once popular as a way of explaining why police forces, including tracker dogs, could never find traces of a big cat despite many members of the public reporting sightings. The idea has largely dropped out of favour as we have learned just how cunning and invisible big cats can be in their native environment – anyone who has seen a BBC wildlife documentary will know how leopards, for one, can remain virtually undetectable even next to a busy African waterhole. On the other hand, the 'phantom cats' notion still bears folkloric fruit – for example, a number of black panther sightings have taken place in locations traditionally associated with appearances by supernatural black dogs. Are the other-worldly varmints shifting their form to keep up with our changing obsessions and expectations?

The third notion about the origin of exotic big cats is rooted in something much more mundane – the law of the land, combined with sheer selfishness. Up until the 1970s anyone could own any kind of creature without a license, and some men with a testosterone overspill thought it was well 'ard to keep a sharp-fanged predator around the house. Then the Dangerous Wild Animals Act was introduced in 1976. This required owners to obtain a local authority license and prove that their pets were adequately caged and cared for. Inevitably, a number of unscrupulous individuals simply released their animals into the wild. A small number also escaped from private zoos.

No one knows how many big cats were dumped in the countryside after 1976. But big cats do not have a lifespan much more than twenty years. Sightings rose enormously in the 1990s and have continued at a high level ever since. These millennium cats cannot be the original crowd; so where have they come from? One simple solution is that additional covert releases have taken place. Environmental consultant Rick Minter, writing in the International Urban *Ecology Review* in 2009, noted that it was common, if unsubstantiated, knowledge among the big cat research community in Britain that lynx were being bred illegally and released so that homegrown hunters could bag 'big game'. Apparently this goes under the name of 'sport'.

But additional releases cannot account for the sheer number and range of sightings. This can only mean that the big cats are breeding, and that we are probably now seeing animals that are third or fourth generation at least. At what point do these cats become an established part of the British ecosystem? Or are they already? Rick Minter's article even speculates that, as with other geographically isolated populations with a limited gene pool, the British big cats might be developing into their own sub-species.

All this makes 'big cats' one of the more exciting aspects of contemporary weirdness. What follows is a more-or-less chronological rundown of sightings in Perth and Kinross, with as much detail on the creatures as can be gleaned from the news reports. Where the story has not come from a newspaper or has been communicated to myself in person, the source is the superb website run by Big Cats in Britain, www.bigcatsinbritain.org.

THE FIRST BIG CAT?

The earliest report I have been able to locate within Perth and Kinross comes from the *Sunday Post* for 15 August 1976. A woman in Glenfarg washing the supper dishes on the evening of 10 August was pestered by her excited pet terrier to be let out. Once out in the garden its barks quickly changed to whimpers, and it stayed stock still shivering with fright. The woman went outside and saw a cat 'the size of a fully grown Labrador' sitting upright on the garden wall. It was at least 3ft tall, with eyes glowing orange in the dark, and its ears were distinctively pointed and tufted. The witness quickly gathered up her terrified dog and ran inside, while the lynx – for that is what it was – spat and howled and then ran off into the neighbouring fields.

It's very likely that this creature was one of those decanted to the countryside in the mass 1976 release. According to the press report, there were claims of other sightings of the beast, including one in Glenfarg's main street, and a suspicion that local chickens were ending up as lynx food.

Following this initial sighting, the records for Perth and Kinross are quiet for almost two decades, even though neighbouring counties such as Angus and Aberdeenshire had a number of sightings. This may mean that no big cats were active in Perthshire at this time, or it may simply be that what sightings there were did not make it to the papers.

THE 1990s

In July 1994 there was a sighting near the A9 at Kindallachan. Sometime in 1995 a large black cat was reported several times in the hills between Loch Rannoch and Glenshee. In August of the same year Mike Guild, Andy Young and three children were camping by Loch Ordie on the Atholl Estate when they were awakened early in the morning by the sounds of something large prowling round the tents. 'I shone my torch and it made a low guttural sound like a big cat, then went off rapidly,' said Mr Guild. He later took photographs and a plaster cast of prints that were 4.5ins long. Note that all these encounters were in Highland Perthshire; big cats can have territories that extend across thirty miles or more, so these may have all been the same animal.

In the year 2000 an anonymous contributor to the Scottish Big Cats website reported a sighting from four years earlier near Bridge of Earn. The witness had been on a Citylink coach from Edinburgh to Perth in late September 1996. From the bus window they spotted what at first was taken to be a horse, but that on second glance proved to be a jet black cat stalking some prey. From its crouching position it darted towards its target, then doubled back as if pursuing a fleeing animal. The witness estimated the animal as being around 5ft long, and reported that a farmer friend in the area had been searching for what had been killing his sheep when he found a small 'den' containing the remains of lamb carcasses.

In 1996 it was Blairgowrie's turn. As reported in the *Daily Mail* for 19 September, local police received several sightings. Around 5 September, Bobby Sommerville, a sixty-nine-year-old retired professor of microbiology, was puzzled when his three Border terriers fled into the house – until he spotted a huge pair of orange eyes at the edge of his floodlit garden. 'I was 20 yards away and I realised I was looking at a huge animal,' he said. 'It sprang away and I could see it was a panther-like creature. It gave a low, snarling growl then escaped into the fields.' Mr Sommerville was in no doubt it was a big cat. The same night, school technician John Stent saw a 'puma-like' animal in his car headlights very close to Mr Sommerville's house, which was outside the town close to the River Ericht. And Ross Shepherd reported that 'something' had been taking piglets from his piggery. The following week there was a pair of sightings around Alyth, and then another in Blairgowrie.

By 1998 the reports coming from across Scotland were so numerous that the issue of big cats was discussed at a conference of high-ranking police officers taking place at the Scottish Police College at Tulliallan Castle in Fife.

MILLENNIAL SIGHTINGS

If Perthshire's big cats had been relatively shy up until now, come the new century they seemed to be positively basking in the limelight. On 27 January the *Courier* reported the experience of Abernyte farmer Graham Anderson, who saw two puma-type animals bounding over a fence dyke. 'I know a wild cat when I see one,' he stated, 'these things were four or maybe six times the size of a wild cat.' On 1 July David Walker and his girlfriend watched a large black cat with a long curled tail, moving low to the ground near the track up from the Spittal of Glenshee hotel to the Dalmunzie hotel, about a mile south of the Glenshee ski area. It was around 10 a.m. on a clear day, and the sighting lasted for about three minutes.

The same month on the B9097 south of Loch Leven a witness named Brian had to brake sharply when a black animal 'about the size of a small Alsatian dog' leaped onto the road in front of him. It was around 11 p.m. and he saw the creature very clearly in the headlights from a distance of 25-30 metres – it had a long and thick body with a rope-like tail, and the combined length of body and tail was greater than the width of the vehicle. The squat head had rounded ears and eyes glowing orange in the light. It did not seem bothered by the car, and after a few seconds leapt over the fence heading south. Brian got out of the car to look for it, then realised that it probably wasn't a good idea to be hanging round on a deserted road looking for large predator, so he headed for the nearest police station to make a report. One of the officers told him his sighting was not the first in the area.

On 3 September 2000 a husband and wife spotted a 'black panther type cat' padding across the path a few yards in front of them on an estate near Errol. All was quiet for a few months then beaters for a pheasant shooting party at Taymount Estate near Stanley disturbed a thin but large black panther-like cat hiding in the dense pinewoods of Green's Landing. One of the three witnesses, trainee gamekeeper Ryan Hurley, told the *Herald* on 28 December, 'It was lying down with its back to me. Then it got up then ran away and hunkered down. It moved with amazing speed through the trees.' One of the shooting party, Glasgow journalist Arnot McWhinnie later saw a four-foot long creature in the same wood. 'I was about 20 yards from it,' he said. 'My first instinct was that it was a very wet fox. Then I dismissed that as I gauged the size of it as it darted in between the trees. It was definitely a big cat.'

In the darkness of a winter's evening in 1999-2000 or 2000-1, a couple travelling north on the A9 near Kindallachan were shocked to see an animal run straight across the road in front of them – so close that they were amazed they did not hit it. In a personal communication of 27 September 2010 they described it as 'Fox-coloured but way too big to be a fox.' They had the definite impression it was feline.

2001

In August 2001 an anonymous witness encountered a large black cat in the coniferous Blackcraig Forest between Ballintuim and Bridge of Cally. The visibility on the summer evening was good and the fifteen-second sighting produced a description of a German Shepherd-sized animal 3ft long with another 2ft of tail, eighteen inches tall, with a 'blunt' head and stomach low to the ground. 'When I saw the animal I clearly remember the hair on the back of my neck standing up and I instinctively picked my dog (a small terrier) up so it wouldn't chase after what I had seen.' On 12 October of the same year a female cyclist named 'J.C.' encountered a 'retriever-sized' black cat on the cycle route between Aberfeldy and Strathtay. The animal had a very long tail and was slowly walking along. The woman was badly frightened and cycled home as quickly as possible. An anonymous correspondent on the Scottish Big Cats site reported a 'black puma' and a sheep kill in the Blairgowrie area on 19 October, while in November Mr H saw a black Labrador-sized cat achieve cheetah-like speed in a field near a filling station in Crook of Devon, and on 11 December two witnesses briefly saw a black cat cross the road in front of their car on the road to Meigle.

2002

There were few reports this year, but all were out of the ordinary. Around 8.30 on an early January morning Mr R witnessed a large fawn-brown muscular cat pad out from a hedge near Scone Palace, jump over a hedge into a field and run south in the direction of Scone. This may be the closest sighting to Perth on record. In July came a highly unusual report from a parent whose ten-year-old son said he had spotted a large black cat out a train window just south of Perth – only the creature was in a cage in the back garden of a house! And in November the

Scottish UFO Casebook website had the briefest of details about an unnamed witness who was reluctant to provide any information other than that he had had to brake suddenly on the A9 south of Pitlochry at 4.30 in the morning – to avoid hitting a lioness… (It is conceivable this could have been a puma or a lynx, as they share a similar colouring).

2003

The sightings for 2003 were all concentrated at the start of the year. At 5.30 in the morning on 10 January a male witness was driving south on the B9099 from Caputh when he saw a 'cougar' with a dark tawny colouring walking up a bank beside the road. On 24 February the *Daily Record* reported that the previous Thursday night four sheep had been killed at a farm in Keillour. One of the kills had been mostly eaten, with a second partially devoured the following night, while wool had been torn off the victims and the rest of the flock was badly spooked. The farmer and a forestry worker caught a brief glimpse of 'something' emerging from the woods but could not identify it. Wildlife officer Allan Stewart commented: 'Generally dogs' claws are pretty blunt and some of the marks look like they could only have been inflicted by a cat. There's no way it could have been a fox but I wouldn't like to say for sure that it was a big cat or dogs.' The final reported sighting of the year came on 15 February, when a driver travelling north on the A9 four miles south of the Birnam junction at 1.30 a.m. had a clear sighting of a dark or black cat standing beside the road. Perhaps 2ft high with a rounded head and visible teeth, it was caught briefly in the headlights.

2005

There appear to have been no sightings from Perth and Kinross in 2004, and only two in 2005, both described in Mark Fraser's *Big Cats in Britain Yearbook 2006*. On 15 July Eoin McDonald had a brief glimpse of a 2ft-high cat as it disappeared into the undergrowth by the B9097 near Kinross, around quarter of a mile west of the RSPB centre at Vane Farm. The tail was long and curved upwards. Mr McDonald had seen a similar animal around three years before, this one about a mile further east. Three days later on 18 July a large black cat was spotted speedily crossing the A90 dual carriageway somewhere southwest of Perth.

2006

Mark Fraser's *Big Cats in Britain Yearbook 2007* gives us four sightings from 2006. In February Karl Simmons had multiple experiences around Ben Lawers above Loch Tay. On Monday the 13th he was out walking when he saw a big black cat with pointed ears; it was around the same size as his Labrador. The following day he, his girlfriend and his son found a fur ball 'the size of his fist' on the other side of the loch some sixteen miles from the location of the sighting. The next day he spotted a deer carcass about 200 yards from where he had first seen the cat, and on the Friday saw a cat-like pawprint five miles away, on the further side of Ben Lawers.

At 8.40 a.m. on 1 July an anonymous witness walking his dog in Bridge of Earn had a close encounter with a black panther-type animal 'the size of a Labrador dog'. At 7.30 p.m. the same day a different man, along with his four-year-old daughter, spent fifteen minutes watching a big cat from as close as 50ft away, in a partly forested agricultural area two miles from Milnathort on the road to Stronachie. The animal seemed to be hunting or stalking prey but when they stopped to watch it, it too ceased its activities and almost seemed to play 'hide and seek' in the grass. When the witness tried to get nearer, the cat sat straight up, with widened eyes and the ears raised, then bounded away into the next field. It was described as the size and colour of a brown Labrador, with a small tail bearing a white outline, and tips or tassels on its ears. As it ran away the ears were pinned back. Once again, this might have been a lynx.

The final sighting documented in the *Yearbook* came on 17 December. A motorist driving up Glen Lednock near Comrie was startled when a big cat 'exploded' out of the woods and leapt from the bank, clearing the road in a single bound before vanishing down the hillside that sloped down to the rover. It must have been running down the slope to achieve such a speed. The sighting was over in flash, leaving the impression of a clear silhouette, in the shape of a cheetah from a wildlife documentary, or the Jaguar emblem from the front of that make of car.

2007

A sighting that may indicate the breeding status of the big cat population took place in June or early July. A thirty-seven-year-old company director was driving from east to west on one of the few straight sections of the A827 on the north shore of Loch Tay, just east of Fearnan, when she spotted two big cat cubs. In a personal communication to me on 27 September 2010 she described them as having a black or dark brown colouring, and padding along one after the other, in the way that kittens do. And although they were definitely young animals, they were far too large to be the offspring of domestic cats or wildcats – each was at least the size of an adult domestic cat, and both had very long tails. The witness did not stop as she had her young child in the car, and although she did not see an adult cat, she had the impression the cubs were following their mother down to the lochside.

2008

In February 'Willie the Gillie' posted a contribution to the website salmonfishingforum.com, stating that a black panther was regularly sighted on a fishing beat of the Tay near Newtyle. He himself had seen prints in the soft earth of a high and near-vertical bank. In leaping up the height the animal had left prints wider than the man's fist, with clear talon scrapes.

2009

2009 proved to be a bumper year for Perthshire's big cats, especially in Strathearn. Early in October retired gamekeeper David McMillan was driving south towards Auchterarder, along the back road from Fowlis Wester to Kinkell Bridge. As he passed the junction with the road to St David's a large black cat trotted across the highway. The publicity generated by the sighting – and which featured a witness who knew his wildlife – encouraged others to report their experiences, and soon the press had dubbed the creature 'the Perthshire puma'. On 10 October the *Courier* carried the story of Lexa McCallum, who actually hit a large black cat as it ran out in front of her car. She had been driving between Auchterarder and Aberuthven at 8 p.m. on a dark night when the accident happened. 'I caught a very brief sight of the animal in my headlights—it was over a metre long and about 18 inches high,' she said. 'It was going at full speed and there was no way I could avoid a collision.' The sixty-eight-year-old instantly stopped and searched the road but there was no sign of the animal, just minor damage to the car in the form of a displaced mudflap. 'I was just amazed by the size of the creature and am absolutely sure it was far big to be any kind of domestic cat.'

Then, on 9 October, the *Strathearn Herald* reported the experience of Oxfordshire man Andrew Feilden who early one morning saw a black panther-like animal at ease in the garden at Tullichettle near Comrie. The sixty-eight-year-old was listened to with respect because he had become familiar with big cats during his three years in Africa. 'This was not any normal British animal. It was the size of a cheetah but had a deeper, thicker body and when it turned its head I could see it was very distinctively feline shaped,' he said. 'It was not flustered and did not seem fearful. Rather it just sat calmly on the lawn. It seemed very contented...When we did let the dogs out they picked up a scent and were sniffing around and it seems the animal had been quite close to the house.' Earlier in September, a Madderty woman and her daughter watched as a large black cat with a distinctive 'panther-like' tail crossed in front of them on the back road to St David's. They came forward only when David McMillan's sighting was reported.

The spate of sightings generated some interesting responses. Alan Stewart, the Wildlife and Environment Officer for Tayside Police, told the *Perthshire Advertiser* on 9 October:

We certainly get an alleged dozen or more big cat sightings reported in Tayside each year varying from black cats resembling panthers to lighter beasts more akin to puma and lynx. I even had a phone call once from a lady convinced that a lion had walked past her. Unfortunately, there is no hard evidence so far to back up such reports.

An otter.
(*The Imperial Dictionary*, 1859)

A binturong, one of the suggested identifications for the Perthshire big cats. This one is in Sydney Zoo. *(Photo by 'sheilaellen', posted on Wikipedia, licensed under the Creative Commons Attribution 2.0 Generic license)*

Local gamekeeper Richard Eadington told the *Strathearn Herald* on 16 October that the culprit was not a cat but actually another animal he had frequently encountered – a large dog (male) otter. 'He's a big bruiser. He plays about the fields and spends a lot of time on open ground and in the Ruchil. When he comes out of the water he's very black from being wet. He's got a broad head and a sweeping tail and could easily be mistaken for a big cat.'

A second alternative creature was identified in the same piece in the *Strathearn Herald* – a binturong, also known as a bearcat (although it is neither bear nor cat, belonging to the civet family). Tree-dwelling omnivores with dark-furred bulky bodies and long bushy prehensile tails that they use to navigate the upper canopy of tropical forests, binturongs are relatively common in South-East Asia, from Bangladesh through Vietnam and Indonesia to the Philippines. Comrie man Neill Aitken had seen many binturongs when he worked in Malaysia. His Perthshire sighting of the critter had taken place in the summer of 2009, but had not been reported until now. He had been walking his dog at the back of Tullichettle when the spooked binturong jumped onto a fence post and then ran across the road, causing a car to brake. Aitken had a clear view of the creature and was in no doubt it was a binturong.

As the photograph shows, a binturong has a superficial resemblance to a big cat, especially if fleetingly glimpsed in a flash encounter. As most people in the UK do not know what a binturong is and what it looks like, it is conceivable that in describing their experience of seeing a strange animal, they plump for a big cat, which are of course more familiar animals, if only through wildlife documentaries and zoo visits. The binturong certainly has the colouring and long tail that is described in many sightings of 'black panthers'. Also the animal eats a mixed diet – fruit, vegetation, eggs, small mammals, birds and anything else it can get. This could go some way to countering one of the persistent criticisms of the 'big cat hypothesis', which questions why so few predator 'kills' are found. Is it possible that one or more binturongs are active in Perthshire? Well, there is an established colony of wallabies on an island in Loch Lomond, and the Lake District has an officially-recognised small population of South American coatimundis, so in theory there is no difficulty in conceiving of an Asian forest-dweller living in the Scottish woodlands. It will be interesting to see if the binturong hypothesis becomes more widespread, and if this in turn brings forward more sightings that specifically identify not a 'big cat' but a 'bearcat'.

In the wild, binturong numbers are declining due to hunting, destruction of their habitats, and cubs being captured for the pet trade. They appear as 'Vulnerable' on the Red List of the International Union for Conservation of Nature and Natural Resources (IUCN). What this means is that the species is facing a high risk of extinction in the wild. Should you wish to acquaint yourself with living binturongs, Edinburgh Zoo has a male (Billy) and a female (Bali).

The *Strathearn Herald* was back on the case on 6 November. Comrie resident Elizabeth Seaward had recently seen a large black animal in broad daylight in a garden near the village's Ross Bridge. The creature had small prick ears, a face bigger than a normal cat's and a long curved tail, with a narrow elegant body and long legs. Although definitely cat-like, Mrs Seaward thought the beast resembled the picture of the binturong the newspaper had printed alongside its story on 16 October. Some two weeks previously a couple from Errol had been driving past Gleneagles at two in the morning when they slowed down to look at a strange creature in the otherwise deserted road. 'What we saw was larger than a Labrador,' said Harry Blair. 'It slowly walked past on the verge, on the passenger side of the car, then it jumped the fence and ran off into the golf course.'

PHYSICAL EVIDENCE?

In my book *Paranormal Dundee* I noted that there had been no reports of big cats in the Dundee and Angus area during the severe winter of 2009-2010, and speculated that the animals may not have survived the harsh conditions. I am pleased to report that no such problem appears to have affected their Perthshire cousins. On 5 February the *Daily Mail* carried a report of

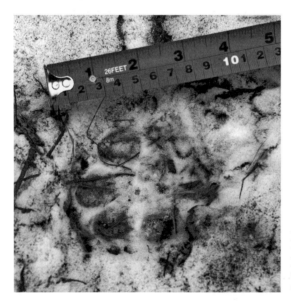

A big cat print in snow, western Perthshire, February 2010: possibly a puma or female leopard, but probably a lynx. (Courtesy of Keith Ringland, www.Ringlandlifeimages.co.uk)

cat-like pawprints found in deep snow on an estate in western Perthshire. Renowned wildlife photographer Keith Ringland of Scone was called out after a gamekeeper tracking roe deer at dusk saw an unusual dark brown shape out of the corner of his eye, and then found the tracks. The deer were noticeably reluctant to enter the wood, which was the opposite of their usual behaviour. Mr Ringland confirmed that a large dog could not have made the prints as dogs cannot retract their claws as cats can, and there were no clawmarks in the prints. Further, at 4ins long, the prints were several times larger than those made by the Scottish wildcat – and the photographer was very familiar with the reclusive native feline. What had made the prints was bigger and heavier than a wildcat. In addition, the gap between the front of one set of paws and the next set of prints was almost 12ft – in other words, the animal had been moving so fast that its bounds were nearly four yards long. The evidence was also well-preserved – melting snow can distort pawprints, changing their apparent shape and size, but in this case the conditions remained so cold that the hard-packed snow retained the original print.

Short of the discovery of an actual animal, these prints may be the best evidence for big cats in Perthshire. Based on his experience, Keith Ringland surmised that the prints had been made by a puma or possibly a female leopard (male leopards have larger prints), but thought the most likely candidate was a lynx.

2010

Once the snows of winter had passed there were more incidents. The *Edinburgh Evening News* for 30 March reported that a sheep had been killed in the Killin area. The significant aspect of this report was that the carcass had been moved some distance and then almost entirely consumed, a behaviour typical of big cats, especially if the original kill-site is too exposed – or if they are feeding cubs. On 6 April an anonymous contributor to the Scottish Big Cats site described a 'large black cat roughly about the size of a Labrador dog' that bounded in front of his car as he was driving through Greenloaning on the Crieff road around 10.15 p.m. The animal crossed the entire width of the road in about three or four strides, so fast that the witness did not even have to brake.

A detailed description of another close encounter was given in the *Courier* on 14 June. Helen Graham of Lower Auchtenny and a friend were driving south along the A912 towards Bridge of Earn, near the Craigend Interchange, at about 11.30 p.m. on the previous Friday night, when something crossed the road in front of them. 'It was definitely cat-like in shape but much bigger than any domestic cat,' she said. 'It had very long, thin legs and a long thin tail and a cat-type face. It had a strange, humped-back look about it and a very convex underside. It was about the size, but not the build, of a spaniel, and it loped slowly across the road and disappeared into the wood below Craigclowan School.' At 8.30 a.m. on 19 July another Scottish Big Cats contributor, Rab Dickson, witnessed a black cat the size of a Labrador cross the road between Kenmore and Aberfeldy. Finally, at 6.45 a.m. on 13 September, Helen Wemyss of Aberuthven saw a 'blacker than black' creature in a field. 'I saw roe deer running and what looked like a jet black bear chasing them,' she told the *Strathearn Herald* on 17 September. 'It was running fast and there were three or four roe deer running away from it. It was about a hundred yards away. The field had just been cut so the animal really stood out.'

SO, ARE THEY OUT THERE?

Some sightings reported above are very probably misidentifications, mistaking feral cats and other local wildlife for something more exotic. And some 'black panthers' may possibly be binturongs (which is just as exciting). But some extended sightings cannot be easily dismissed, and, combined with physical evidence such as the pawprints shown, this leads to the cautious conclusion that Perthshire is very probably home to a small breeding population of big cats. 'Hot spots' seem to include the area from Bridge of Earn south into Kinross-shire; Strathearn from Auchterarder up to Comrie; the western part of Highland Perthshire; and from the Carse of Gowrie up towards the Blairgowrie area.

As to what species the creatures are, that will have to wait for more physical evidence. I'm reasonably confident that lynx are present, possibly as a result of recent covert releases; are New World pumas and African-Asian leopards also stalking the hills and straths, or are other creatures also in our midst?

A CAUTIONARY TALE

We finish this chapter with a tale passed to me by a correspondent who wished to remain anonymous. It concerns incidents at the outdoor centre in Highland Perthshire. Many years ago, so the story goes, a headstrong horse-riding instructor named Sabrina had worked at the centre. With long dark hair, sharp purple fingernails and a personality that preferred her vicious black cat and the centre's small collection of horses to the company of humans, she was decidedly unpopular with the kids. After one too many complaints she had a massive row with the boss and stormed off in the middle of the night. Blinded by rage, she did not pay attention to her driving and the car left the muddy track, hitting a tree at full speed. Sabrina died instantly under the light of the full moon.

Early the following morning the baker found the burnt-out car. But there was no body. Police hunted high and low but somehow the body had been removed from the burning vehicle, and it was never found.

Exactly a month later, the horses at the centre were attacked, one suffering scratches so deep the vet had to be called. He was deeply puzzled at the wounds, as they could only have been made by a large clawed animal ... such as a big cat. On each of the following nights either side of the full moon more attacks took place, and the feeling developed that the camp was a dangerous place to be at night. Sabrina's cabin lay empty and started to develop a reputation... the kids avoided it, even in the daytime.

After the centre closed for the summer, rumours started to circulate among the local gamekeepers and farmers. Partially eaten deer carcasses were found. Chickens and lambs went missing. Horses turned up with deep scratch marks down their flanks. Could a big cat be on the prowl?

The following year the camp opened as usual. One night, horrible, inhuman screams were heard. Staff and children felt they were being watched. The kids whispered about ghosts and scary animals in the woods. The name Sabrina appeared on several lips. The next day staff decided to impose a curfew after dark. Anyone needing the toilet had to be accompanied by an adult and they had to carry whistles and torches if they left the cabins. That night the athletic twenty-year-old sailing instructor escorted a little lad to the latrine block, and waited outside. Out of the darkness came a low, menacing snarl. The man was never seen again…

The trail of blood and shredded clothes led into the dark pinewoods. The police and the Territorial Army combed the area but no corpse was ever found. The centre was closed, and remained so for many years. In the decades since, the occasional hillwalker has gone missing. Like the murder of the staff member, the deaths were hushed up so as not to affect the tourist trade. Deer are still found slaughtered, and sightings of big cats in the area have been on the increase. A predator still stalks the hills, and now the outdoor centre has been re-opened, the creature may find easier prey in the form of unsuspecting children staying at summer camp…

There is a strange coda to the story. A few years ago, long after the initial scandal had died down, two local farmers were out trying to catch a fox that had been taking their lambs. It was a full moon, and at the far end of the field they saw what they thought was a very large fox. One of them fired and hit it – and then the two men watched as the creature stood up on its hind legs and ran off with a gait that resembled both a female human and a big cat – and flowing behind it was a mane of long dark hair…

The full moon and the transformed creature all borrow from classic werewolf themes, but apart from this mythic element, could the story's inclusion of big-cat elements be related to something authentic? Well, no. As my correspondent gleefully noted, this story has been doing the rounds among the staff of outdoor centres in Scotland and the USA for decades now, with the details being adapted to each location. It is typically told by a teacher sitting round a campfire, and you can imagine the effect it has on the city kids as they huddle round the fire, surrounded by the darkness of the unfamiliar woods. In one sense it is just a good scary ghost story, the perfect accompaniment to a day and night spent in the outdoors. On the other hand, it also functions as what folklorists call a 'cautionary tale'. If the children even suspect that there might be a big cat out there prepared to drag them off, they will pay great attention to their surroundings. And on the potentially hazardous Scottish hills, that is no bad thing.

My informant – someone well-known in outdoor education – told me that the story of Sabrina was currently being told at several outdoor centres in Highland Perthshire. I wonder – how much is the circulation of the tale contributing to sightings of big cats? Are we seeing living folklore in action?

TWO

UFOS – AND OTHER STRANGE THINGS IN THE SKIES

'One repeating mystery – the mystery of the local sky.'

Charles Fort, *New Lands*.

Since the term 'flying saucers' was coined in 1947, the news media, popular culture and the general public alike have been gaga for tales of sightings of what are alleged to be extraterrestrial visitors. From the 1990s, with the global popularity of *The X-Files*, Unidentified Flying Objects have been continually popular, the obsession fuelled by the internet and the tender ministrations of the British tabloids, some of which, it seems, would print a picture of an out-of-focus Frisbee if it allowed them to get the word 'UFO' in the headline.

As astronomy professionals and other scientists and rationalists wearily point out, most sightings of 'UFOs' are really 'IFOs', that is, Identified Flying Objects. A surprising number of people misidentify things in the sky. The most common culprits for 'UFO sightings' are: helicopters; other aircraft; balloons and dirigibles; the planet Venus (which is both the Evening Star and the Morning Star, depending on its orbit and position to the Sun); the bright star Sirius; the moon (particularly when seen through clouds); searchlights and car headlights reflected off low cloud; birds; lenticular (saucer-shaped) clouds; satellites; the International Space Station, which is the third brightest object in the sky after the sun and moon; flares; meteors; and Chinese (or Thai) fire lanterns released at celebrations and other events.

However, when all the likely suspects are eliminated, there are still a small number of cases that remain mysterious. But before we consider the unknown let us look at the known, those elements of the natural or human world that can that bamboozle anyone who watches the skies. Many of these known factors are themselves strange and full of wonder.

BOMBARDMENT FROM SPACE

Each day our planet is bombarded with hundreds of small pieces of space debris – the dust bunnies of the vacuum of space. Most are tiny and burn up in the atmosphere without anyone noticing. A minority have a noticeable flare as they streak across the night skies, creating the classic 'shooting star' or meteor. A miniscule fraction of these meteors make it to the ground surface, creating meteorites – physical evidence of our continuing assault from space. Most meteorites are very small, the majority of their mass having been burned off during their journey through our thankfully thick atmosphere. Only a handful have any appreciable size.

All of which makes Loch Leven possibly unique on the planet. Because something like 300 million years ago a large asteroid was sucked in by the Earth's gravitational pull and plunged through our atmosphere. Most meteorites disintegrate on impact, but this massive chunk of space rock hit the ground at a low angle, causing it to 'bounce' off the surface and break into fragments, two of which acted like 'skipping stones' and landed in Gargunnock and Bannockburn in Stirlingshire. In each case the impact created a large crater, the extremely high-pressure shockwave melting rocks and transferring elements and compounds from outer space. Over the many millions of years erosion wore away the crater walls, leaving only the crater surfaces and their unusual geological structures. Loch Leven, which has the shape of an ellipse eight miles long and three miles across, is the eroded basin of the largest crater. The only other similar low-angle impact craters known are on the moon (which has two) and Mars (which manages three). The Loch is the only place non-astronauts can go to visit such a crater.

The asteroid's geological fingerprint was recognised by Kinross scientist Dr Brendan Hamill in 2003, and revealed at a conference organised by the Lunar and Planetary Institute in Germany that year. Speaking to the press, Dr Hamill said the geology of Loch Leven could help research into the evolution of the solar system, 'and may provide an insight into the possibility of extraterrestrial life'. In one of the scientific abstracts provided for the conference, he notes that several other impact craters from around the world of a different type may all date from the same period. The consequences of these major impacts may have annihilated Laurentia and Laurussia, the vast primeval forests of the Carboniferous Era that blanketed much of the Northern Hemisphere. In this sense the Loch Leven impact was as significant as the later asteroid strike that probably wiped out the dinosaurs 65 million years ago, and makes the famously devastating asteroid explosion over Tunguska in Siberia in 1908 look like a kid's firecracker.

Fortunately, most space visitors are less destructive, although some can still pack a punch. In 1767 *The Annual Register: A View Of The History, Politics, And Literature For The Year* recorded a fireball that came in at a low angle, knocking a man off his horse, carrying a large cart in its slipstream, destroying half of a house and taking out an arch of the new bridge at Blairgowrie. On 19 November 1791 a fireball as large as the full moon lit up the night sky over Clunie, splitting into two smaller pieces and then exploding with a great noise just above the horizon (the incident is in the *Old Statistical Account of 1791-1799*). On 3 December 1917 another fireball detonated over the Sidlaw Hills, raining meteorite fragments over the area. Four substantial pieces were recovered, three in Perthshire – at Easter Essendy (22lb 4oz/9.9kg), Cairsie (2lb 6oz/1085gm), and Keithick (2lb 8oz/1172gm) – and one in Angus at South Corston (2lb 5oz/1141gm). All four pieces of the 'Strathmore Meteorite' are on display in the Perth Museum and Art Gallery on George Street.

The Keithick fragment crashed through the roof of a building near Coupar Angus, while at Cairsie a local woman saw the meteorite hit the ground just 20m from where she was standing, such eye-witness accounts of meteorite strikes being very rare. Yet according to the *American Journal of Science* a similar episode may have taken place near Crieff on 23 April 1855. The facts of the case could not be definitely uncovered, but it seems a young woman staying at Ochtertyre House saw a luminous object fall to the ground, and picked it up, but then dropped it (either because it was hot, or because she thought it was hot). Perhaps another eleven further fragments 'emitting a sulphurous odour' had fallen nearby. (Charles Fort gathered the accounts in his book *New Lands*.)

Further meteorites landed near Loch Tay (15 September 1802), on the North Inch of Perth (17 May 1830), and (probably) in the area of Milnab Street and Carrington Terrace, Crieff (22 August 1997). Meanwhile, exceptionally bright meteors were seen at Coupar Angus (18 August 1783), Bendochy (1790s), Meigle (15 July 1871), and over Abernyte, Pitlochry, Longforgan, Madderty and Perth (27 December 1973).

PHANTOM AIRSHIPS

In the later years of the nineteenth century and the early years of the twentieth century, people did not look up into the skies and 'see' alien spaceships. Instead they looked up into the skies and 'saw' airships. And they saw those gas-filled aircraft in places where no airships could possibly be. From the Great Plains of America to the pampas of Argentina, reports flooded in of giant airships, foreign spies descending from the clouds, aerial saboteurs and other strange intrusions from the sky. None were confirmed by any reputable authority. Later researchers have dubbed the phenomenon the 'Phantom Airship' mystery, or the 'Scareship Mystery'.

With the outbreak of the First World War, the pre-existing 'scareship' trope was amplified by war fever and panic over aerial attacks. Despite the fact that German Zeppelins only had enough fuel capacity to reach limited parts of eastern and south-eastern England, the enemy airships were 'sighted' up and down the British Isles, including the west coast – and Scotland. Zeppelins and other enemy aircraft were reported in Dumfries and Galloway, Ayrshire, the Firth of Forth, Aberdeenshire, Elgin, the Banff coast, Badenoch, Lochaber, Dornoch, Wick, Gruinard Bay and even the Western Isles. The vast majority of these reports came from the hours of darkness or twilight, and many involved not descriptions of actual aircraft but strange lights and noises. When it was pointed out that no German machine could reach these places from the Continent, a rumour spread that secret supply bases must have been established in remote areas. The authorities took this seriously, and posters offering a reward of £100 were put up in many country areas. They warned citizens to be on the look out for 'a secret base in some unfrequented part of Scotland where they are able to obtain supplies of oil, petrol and other stores. Such a base would probably consist of a store of oil and petrol concealed in an unfrequented locality, possibly in the charge of an armed caretaker.' Suspicion was focused on sites in Nairnshire and Galloway, while a nest of spies was said to be operating near Fraserburgh. All these rumours and more have been collected in a splendid book edited by Nigel Watson, *The Scareship Mystery: A Survey of Worldwide Phantom Airship Scares*.

The Perthshire experience of the scare has been catalogued in Malcolm Fife's book *Scottish Aerodromes of the First World War*. In November 1914 *The People's Journal* commented that Atholl had been at the centre of rumours about both enemy aircraft and spies, claiming that many people believed a secret German airfield was operating in the Perthshire Highlands. For three or four nights between 8.15 and 9.15 p.m. an airship was sighted flying north through the main glen that also takes the road and railway. Its red, green and white lights flashed in a regular sequence, a clear indication of covert communications with the ground. 'On one of the evenings the air vessel whose form could not be distinguished against the enveloping background of a murky sky was sighted by a number of young men who were in the vicinity of Moulin. They were convinced that no astronomical proposition could account for the presence of the unusual aerial visitant. Following its course with anxious and straining eyes they were amazed to note the unusual night voyager drop suddenly and so near at hand to appear to alight on Pitlochry golf course on the slopes of Craiglunie. But the finality of the descent had been only apparent on account of the imperfect perspective and no trace of the craft was to be found.' A short time later a 'searchlight' passed over Mid Atholl from the lower part of the Tummell Valley, its bright beam clearly illuminating houses as it swept along the northern slopes of the glen.

Whatever people were seeing, or thought they were seeing, they were certainly not airships, as no German craft could have reached that far, and no military or private aircraft were operating in the area. Thorough searches found no trace of a fuel cache or secret base. By the summer of 1915 the 'airship scare' had largely fizzled out, but for around eleven months at the start of the war it had gripped the British imagination.

To put these rumours into perspective, we must consider the tense atmosphere of the times, with a genuine fear of invasion prompting anxiety, speculations and delusions. In the first week of the war, for example, everyone 'knew' that a great sea battle had taken place in the North Sea. Despite no such conflict having taken place, eyewitnesses came forward to say they had personally seen the battleships fighting, and a steamer captain reported with great sincerity that he had seen the masts of nineteen sunken German warships, protruding from the shallow waters where they lay. In the light of these and many similar untruths, each deeply believed in at the time, it is reasonable to conclude that the 'phantom airships' of 1914 were simply ordinary or mundane phenomena misinterpreted through the distorting lens of war fever. It would not be the last time that psychological factors played a role in generating anxiety about strange things in the sky.

GREETINGS PERTH-LINGS!

In recent years the Ministry of Defence has been regularly releasing batches of its 'UFO files' into the public domain, by making them accessible from the National Archives. The documents contain the reports made by the general public to the RAF and police concerning sightings of unusual things in the sky. The MoD has consistently maintained that its sole interest in this topic is to ascertain if the reports have any defence significance; outside the possibility that the sightings are of Russian 'bogeys' or other intrusions into UK air space, the chaps at the ministry claim no interest in the UFO question.

The batch of records released in 2007 contain six sightings from the night of 14 September 2005, all from people who contacted the police, RAF or the Met Office from across Fife and Perthshire. At 8:50 p.m. a resident of Letham in Fife called about 'White circles all over the sky'. Five minutes later a Blairgowrie witness reported 'Three white circles going clockwise then anti-clockwise'. At 9.15 p.m. someone from Lochgelly reported 'Bright, white lights that were moving in semi circles'. At 9.23 a call came in from Kinross concerning two or three 'Bright green and luminous lights circling'. Twenty-two minutes later a Glenrothes resident saw 'three to six bright, white lights in circles'. And at 11.15 a caller from Crieff described 'Clear-white lights, like a torch but no beam'.

The Horsecross Concert Hall, Perth. Its opening ceremony in 2005 sparked many UFO reports. *(Photo by Geoff Holder)*

Was it an ET jamboree? Had the invasion from Mars begun? Actually, no. As virtually all the national press on 16 September reported, the lights had simply been the spectacular searchlight performance marking the opening of Perth's swish new Horsecross concert hall. The ten-light display, created by artist Simon Wilkinson, could be seen for miles in the clear atmospheric conditions. A spokesman for Fife Police commented: 'The lights could be seen as far away as Kinglassie and Lochgelly. People were quite worried – several callers thought it was UFOs.' The newspapers vied for the best alien-related headline. The *Daily Express* came close with 'Panic on day that Perth stood still' (a reference to the sci-fi film *The Day the Earth Stood Still*), but the prize goes to an anonymous headline writer on *The Sun* – 'Greetings Perth-lings'.

More party lights provoked a UFO response in 2008. Each autumn a patch of woodland at Faskally near Pitlochry is given over to a sound and light show entitled the Enchanted Forest. As reported in the *Daily Record* for 25 October, the attraction's lightshow prompted a UFO report. Part of the popular event that year featured an 'ET Wood' with inflatables of 'little green men'. Within a short time two thirds of the foot-high toys had disappeared. Spokeswoman Tricia Fox commented, 'We started with 100 inflatables but over the past few days their number has been depleted. Either people are swiping them as souvenirs or it's a case of ET goes home.'

A PLAGUE OF FIRE LANTERNS

Chinese or Thai fire lanterns have become increasingly popular in recent years, being set off at birthdays, weddings, New Year's celebrations and many other occasions. A small fuel source is ignited within a fragile paper frame held together by wires; the heat from the flame expands the air within the lantern causing it to rise up, and the flame combined with the thin coloured

Fire lanterns at the Khom Fai festival, Thailand. *(Photo by 'Takeaway', posted on Wikipedia, licensed under the Creative Commons Attribution-Share Alike 3.0 Unported license)*

paper creates the distinctive orange glowing effect. I was once at a music festival where dozens were released into the sky from within the audience, prompting some interesting reactions from the more, er, enhanced revellers. The glowing spheres are responsible for dozens upon dozens of UFO sightings, the typical description being of several orange lights moving silently through the skies. The lights may also 'mysteriously' disappear — which is what happens when the flame simply runs out of fuel. Although lovely to look at, they do pose a potential environmental hazard. The remains of the metal-and-paper frame can be ingested by farm animals and wildlife, causing digestive distress or even death, and the still-hot fragments could ignite heather or grass when they fall to earth.

A quick round-up of reports on the invaluable www.uk-ufo.co.uk website reveals sightings of silent orange lights over Dunkeld (31 August 2007), north-east of Perth (1 February 2008), Perth (2 September and 4 October 2008), Kinloch Rannoch (31 December 2008 – Hogmanay), outside Alyth (1 January 2009 - ditto), Blairgowrie (1 February 2009), Muthill (14 February 2009 – Valentine's Day), Blair Atholl (15 April and 18 April 2009), Aberfeldy (24 December 2009 – Christmas Eve), Grandtully (1 January 2010 – New Year's), Blairgowrie (16 January 2010), Perth (18 January 2010), Crieff (24 January 2010), Crieff and Braco (4 April 2010), Dunkeld (17 April 2010) and 'Perthshire' (5 August 2010). There have no doubt been many more. In Perthshire as elsewhere, fire lanterns have numerically dominated UFO reports since the mid-2000s, and being in groups and relatively slow-moving they are reasonably easy to capture on mobile phone cameras — something that has been greatly appreciated by tabloid newspapers, which delight in printing colour pictures of glowing orange 'alien invaders'. Sigh. Phantom airships were much more exciting.

'LITS' – LIGHTS IN THE SKY

The late cataloguer of the strange, John A. Keel (author of *The Mothman Prophecies*, among many similar works) coined the acronym LITS for 'Lights in the Sky'. Leaving aside all the sources noted in the preceding paragraphs, the typical UFO report does indeed consist of little more than LITS. Very rarely is any kind of structured craft observed. Some of these LITS sightings very likely have a prosaic explanation. For example, take three sightings communicated to the UK-UFO website. A report of 22 September 2009 from Blairgowrie described a very bright satellite-like light that went dark then bright again, the cycle repeating between 4 and 5.30 a.m. At a guess this was the International Space Station, which is not only extremely bright, being very large and reflective, but also has numerous extensions that can reflect sunlight at different angles. Similarly, a sighting of a very bright white light moving steadily eastwards over Crieff at 4.45 a.m. on 31 August of the same year was almost certainly the ISS. And either the ISS or another satellite very likely accounted for a sighting from 15 December 2009 over Fearnan, of a 'star' moving silently and slowly eastwards in the pre-dawn sky at 7.18 a.m. The same explanation may account for one of the reports released by the MoD, of a bright object moving in a similar trajectory to a satellite, which brightened during the period of observation over Blairgowrie on 17 March 2000. Another declassified document from the Ministry of Defence files mentions an orange 'ball of fire with a tail' seen dropping down to the horizon from the Coupar Angus/Blairgowrie area at 7.50 p.m. on 5 October 1997. The description is too imprecise to suggest a definitive explanation, but it may have been the ISS, a meteor, or perhaps a piece of spacecraft junk (such as a satellite delivery rocket) burning up as it entered the atmosphere.

By and large aerial objects that display flashing lights are likely to be helicopters or other aircraft (the standard night-flying system is a combination of rotating red and green lights with flashing white strobes). The appearance of the aircraft is sometimes distorted by atmospheric conditions, poor light or distance. So, for instance, the Ministry of Defence files include a member of the public's sighting of something with five flashing lights underneath and more on the side (seen over Perth on the night of 17 March 2000) and a 'cigar-shaped' object bearing a bright white light, two red lights and a pulsating red light (seen over Almondbank at 4.40 p.m. on 24 November 2000). Another aircraft was probably responsible for the report in the *Courier* of 3 February 2000, which described the experience of an Inchyra man who had seen a silver object with four or five black markings on the side flying over the Carse of Gowrie the previous week.

MYSTERY OBJECTS?

If we filter out sightings that appear to originate with natural phenomena, light shows, lanterns, satellites or aircraft, we are still left with a small core of genuinely puzzling events, most of which feature aerial objects performing near-impossible manoeuvres.

Four reports submitted to the UK-UFO website mention behaviour of this kind. On 12 December 2009 and on two previous occasions a witness from Trinafour saw 'two very bright stars' adjacent to each other at 7.30 a.m. in the pre-dawn winter sky. Small lights were passing between them as if they were connected by a 'bike chain'. After about three minutes the two main lights flew apart and moved in opposite directions. On one occasion one of the lights was flashing. It is conceivable this was some kind of mid-air refuelling exercise involving a military aircraft and a tanker plane, but what are we to make of the following three incidents submitted to the same site?

At 10.30 p.m. on 27 July 2008, three people watched as a bright glowing object hovered over Auchterarder, then moved north at a steady constant speed, and finally accelerated at an incredible rate, to vanish into the distance within two to three seconds. It was a cloudless clear night with good visibility and they watched the undetermined object through binoculars. The three were adamant it was not a military jet or a helicopter. On the final night of 2008 a man in Errol spotted an orange 'shuttlecock' descending towards him. Initially the date and colour would suggest a fire lantern, but the object ceased its descent, came to a stop, and then split in two – with the head zooming off to the northeast faster than an aeroplane and the body travelling equally fast to the east, while climbing rapidly. And at 9 p.m. on 12 August 2009 a witness spotted a bright red light moving at speed across the Ochil Hills. The light came to a sudden stop and then vertically ascended to what the witness described as 'to the height of a space station'. It remained stationary at this high altitude for several minutes, then a second red light came into view lower down, to the left of the original light. At this point both lights disappeared.

If the observations are accurate, the acceleration, change of direction and manoeuvrability of the objects go beyond most of our current technology. I have a sneaking suspicion that at least one of the sightings is a misidentified Harrier, the 'jump jet' that can hover and take off vertically as well as operate like a normal jet fighter. But this can't be the explanation for all the sightings. What are people witnessing?

DIAMONDS ARE A UFO-SPOTTER'S BEST FRIEND

One clue to the mystery may be found in what has become to be known as 'The Pitlochry Incident'. On the other hand, the story seems to raise as many questions as it answers, so it may be a solution – or it may be another layer of confusion and obfuscation to add to the mystery.

The incident took place at 9 p.m. on 4 August 1990, over Calvine, on the A9, twenty miles north of Pitlochry. Two men witnessed a diamond-shaped craft hover in the same position for ten minutes before ascending vertically upwards at high speed. They stated a military aircraft was also in the area making a series of low-level passes. The witnesses took a number of colour photographs which were sent to the *Daily Record* in Glasgow. The newspaper did not run the images but passed the six negatives to the Ministry of Defence.

What happened next was finally revealed when the files were declassified by the MoD in March 2009. Normally the Government expressed no interest in UFO sightings unless they appeared to be of defence significance. But the Calvine photographs set off all sorts of alarm bells. So much so, that the Ministry of Defence officials felt compelled to warn their political masters, because they believed the images would mean that Ministers would soon be asked questions about them by the media, or even in Parliament. 'Such stories are not normally drawn to the attention of Ministers and the MoD press office invariably responds to questions along well-established lines emphasising our limited interest in the UFO phenomenon,' stated the briefing memo prepared for Sir Archie Hamilton, the then Armed Forces Minister, on

14 September 1990. However, the memo continued, 'They [the photographs] show a large stationary, diamond-shaped object past which, it appears, a small jet aircraft is flying.'

A large, stationary, diamond-shaped object. It apparently had no wings and no visible propulsion system. It could hover for ten minutes and depart at speed. It was the working definition of an impossible aircraft. So what was it?

The spooks at the Ministry suspected that what had been snapped was in fact an Aurora, an allegedly ultra-top-secret American stealth bomber that could fly at hypersonic speeds. Since the late 1980s the UFO world had been afire with rumours of such a 'black' project, and by 1991 both popular publications and specialist aviation journals (such as *Jane's Defence Weekly*) were awash with 'Aurora fever'. The craft was supposed to be able to attain Mach 8 (that is, eight times faster than the speed of sound), with a top speed of 5,300mph. It would have been the fastest thing on the planet, outstripping the F-117 Nighthawk fighter and B-2 Spirit bomber, the swept-back wings of which are now familiar from Hollywood movies.

But if Aurora was real, the Americans weren't telling their supposed closest ally; and the MoD were of the opinion that the US was secretly testing the project in UK airspace – without as much as a by-your-leave to the British Government. The released MoD files show that officials assiduously collected cuttings from magazines and newspapers relating to the Aurora rumours. Attached to one article from September 1991 was an official's personal note: 'Attention is really focusing on this now, notwithstanding a recent USAF (US Air Force) 'denial briefing'. This is bound to prompt further questions/Parliamentary interest.' The civil servants of department DI55 of the Defence Intelligence Staff also scoured reports by air traffic controllers and RAF and commercial pilots in search of sightings of similarly-shaped aircraft. It is ironic, is it not, that a department set up to assess Russian military threats and incursions was obsessed with American violations of British airspace. After a year of investigation, however, the MoD could come to no conclusion about the Calvine diamond, and the photographs were returned to the newspaper. The following year (1992) defence officials commissioned an artist to produce line drawings of the original photographs, suggesting someone in the Ministry was still intrigued.

A member of the public requested release of the documents under the Freedom of Information Act, and The Ministry of Defence response included the following information:

> Two members of the public contacted *The Scottish Daily Record* to report a large diamond shape UFO hovering for about 10 minutes before ascending vertically upwards at high speed. The witnesses said that during the sighting an RAF aircraft believed to be a Harrier was in the area. The sighting was over Calvine, 20 miles north of Pitlochry at 2100 hours on 4 August 1990. A number of colour photographs were taken and passed to *The Scottish Daily Record*, who in turn sent the negatives to the MOD. These were considered at the time and it was concluded that the jet was a Harrier. No definite conclusions were reached regarding the large diamond-shaped object. Our records show that the original negatives were returned to *The Scottish Daily Record*.

The failure of the MoD to define the diamond-shaped craft in the photo may suggest to some that what had been captured was the advanced technology of an alien race. But perhaps it's time to apply Occam's Razor, a very useful piece of analytical advice formulated by the medieval philosopher William of Occam. The Razor comes in various forms, typically

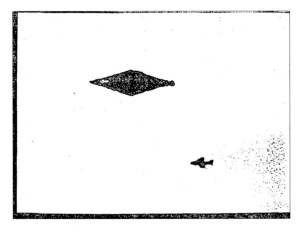

The mysterious diamond-shaped craft allegedly seen over Calvine in 1990. *(The National Archives, DEFE 31/180/1)*

expressed something like: 'No more things should be presumed to exist than are absolutely necessary', or 'Do not multiply entities unnecessarily'. In other words, all other things being equal, the simplest solution is the most likely. Occam's Razor does not deny the possibility of the extraordinary (such as alien spacecraft) but it does suggest the solution to a particular mystery is more likely to have an ordinary cause (such as natural phenomena or human action).

There are two clues in the 1990 episode. The first is that, despite the tabloid hunger for UFO stories, the *Daily Record* did not publish the photographs, and I can find no record in the released MoD files that suggests an official ban was placed on publication. So why did the paper not run the story? The photographs appear to no longer exist – or at least their whereabouts are unknown – and all that remains is the blurry photocopy in the MoD files. The second clue is the smaller aircraft in the photograph. The MoD identified this as a Harrier, but they could not track down any record of such a warplane being in the air above Perthshire on that date. According to the RAF, no Harrier was flying above Calvine on 4 August 1990. And then there's the slight inconvenience that, despite all the speculation, there is no evidence whatsoever that the alleged diamond-shaped Aurora ever existed.

And so we come to the crux of the matter: are the Calvine pictures actually reliable? In point of fact, there is no record that the unnamed photographer was ever interviewed by anyone in authority. The MoD appears to have taken the photos at face value … but could they be a hoax?

In the end the sighting remains an enigma. Proof of a secret black project that is so covert it is still under wraps? Photographic evidence of an alien spacecraft? Or a clever fake?

'I THINK WE'RE BEING FOLLOWED…'

In a small number of cases witnesses claim that a UFO follows them for some distance when they are driving. For instance, Ron Halliday's *UFO Scotland* mentions the experience of a couple on a skiing holiday in Glenshee (probably in 1984) who were followed by a bright disc-shaped object for four miles along the A93. At the end of the encounter the object moved upwards at a great speed. A similar experience happened to James Wannan and his wife in 1967. On a dark December evening they were driving southeast along the narrow, dangerous minor road that runs from Kenmore towards Amulree. Where the road tops the pass that leads into lonely Glen Quaich it reaches a height of 1,736ft (529m) above sea level. At the time the Wannans were living at Tirchardie Farm, one of the few buildings in the glen. As he negotiated the twists and turns Mr Wannan noticed that his wife was becoming agitated and distressed. When he asked her what was wrong, she pointed up to the sky.

Clearly visible against the night sky was a cigar-shaped, elongated cylinder, coloured a bright candy-pink. As the car continued its journey, the object followed them, being clearly visible throughout. This carried on for perhaps five or six miles. At one point Mr Wannan stopped and got out of the car to inspect the strange object – which then became stationery itself. The farmer noticed it gave off a very low-pitched hum, almost like a vibration. By now Mrs Wannan was very distraught, so her husband set off for home. As the car crossed an old iron bridge over the River Quaich, just before Tirchardie, the object disappeared.

James Wannan is now deceased. The story was given to me in a personal communication by his son, Scott Fraser. Scott remembers his father recounting the episode in crisp detail. In addition, many years later James Wannan, now an old man and retired, returned to Glen Quaich to catch up about the old times with a gamekeeper who lived near the head of the glen. During their reminiscences the subject of the strange sighting came up. The gamekeeper (who sadly has also passed away) volunteered that he too had seen something unusual moving through the sky around the same time. His clearest memory was that it was bright pink.

In June or July 1994, Scott Fraser and his partner spent a night camping at the top of the glen. It was a bright, clear evening with no cloud, and being close to the Summer Solstice there was still light in the sky this far north, so the couple went for a walk around 11.20 p.m. The views over the heather moorlands and hills were expansive. While admiring the view they both saw a 'phosphorus-bright' object moving erratically around the sky, from left to right, then up and down, and covering two to three miles of open sky faster than any man-made object. Scott described the object's manoeuvrability as 'breathtaking' and was convinced it outperformed the most advanced aircraft. His opinion carries weight because he is an aeronautical engineer, and was familiar with high-performance military aircraft such as the Typhoon Eurofighter, F16s and so on. In his view it was faster and more manoeuvrable than anything he had ever seen. There was no beam of light from the ground, and he was convinced it was a definite structured object. During the sighting, which lasted for perhaps two or three minutes, the 'whiter than white' object kept to an average estimated height of 1,000ft, sometimes shooting up to perhaps twice that height and then plunging down vertically. It may have been a sphere, but its speed and abrupt changes of direction sometimes created the impression of a cylinder, so Scott was unsure as to the actual shape. At the end of the sighting the painfully bright mystery object shot upwards and left their sight. The incident had taken place at or near the same spot that Scott's parents had had their encounter, some twenty-seven years previously.

THREE

THE HAUNTING OF
BALLECHIN HOUSE

'What you do in this world is a matter of no consequence... The question is, what can you make people believe that you have done.'

Sherlock Holmes in *A Study in Scarlet*, by Sir Arthur Conan Doyle.

These days Ballechin is a scatter of modern buildings on a private off-limits estate above the A827 that runs through Strathtay. Nothing remains of Ballechin House, the mansion that was at the heart of a Victorian supernatural *cause célèbre*, a scandal that split the Society for Psychical Research and gripped the readers of *The Times*, then very much the newspaper of the upper echelons of society. The storm broke in 1897, but there were earlier stirrings of strange goings on, and these need to be understood because they feed into the main narrative of extraordinary hauntings, apparitions, messages from the other side, and a whole host of further supernatural phenomena. With the house now long gone, our best visual guide to the location are the four floor plans used in *The Alleged Haunting of B-------- House*, published in 1899 by Ada Goodrich Freer and Lord Bute, and reproduced here. As well as this primary source, two essential works on the subject are *Strange Things*, by John L. Campbell and Trevor H. Hall, and Mr Hall's *The Strange Case of Ada Goodrich Freer*.

THE ALLEGED HAUNTING

OF

B—— HOUSE

INCLUDING

A JOURNAL KEPT DURING THE TENANCY OF
COLONEL LEMESURIER TAYLOR

EDITED BY

A. GOODRICH-FREER (Miss X)

AND

JOHN, MARQUESS OF BUTE, K.T.

LONDON
GEORGE REDWAY
1899

The title page of *The Alleged Haunting of B—— House. (Author's Collection)*

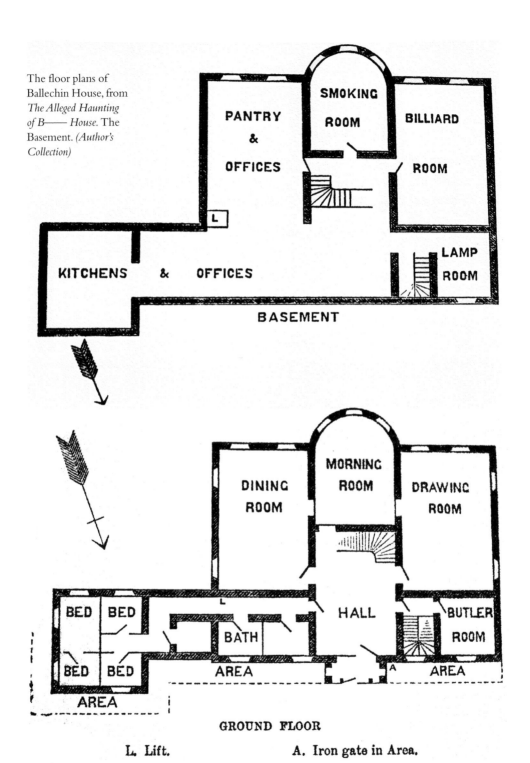

The floor plans of Ballechin House, from *The Alleged Haunting of B—— House.* The Basement. *(Author's Collection)*

PANTRY & OFFICES

SMOKING ROOM

BILLIARD ROOM

L

KITCHENS & OFFICES

LAMP ROOM

BASEMENT

DINING ROOM

MORNING ROOM

DRAWING ROOM

BED BED

L

BATH

HALL

BUTLER ROOM

BED BED

AREA

A AREA

AREA

GROUND FLOOR

L. Lift.   **A. Iron gate in Area.**

The Ground Floor. *(Author's Collection)*

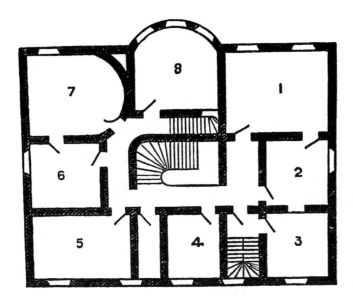

SECOND FLOOR

The upper floor with the bedrooms. Room 8 seemed to be the focus of many of the incidents. *(Author's Collection)*

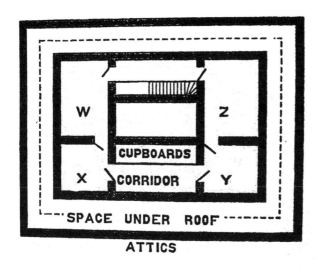

ATTICS

The top floor. One guest found a crawl-through passage here. *(Author's Collection)*

THE BEGINNINGS

Ballechin House was built in 1806, on the site of a property that had been the ancestral home of the prominent Steuart family for centuries. A wing extension was added in the 1880s. The Steuarts had had a distinguished role in Scottish politics and warfare since the 1500s. In 1825 Robert Steuart, the nineteen-year-old heir, set out to the East to seek his fortune, eventually attaining the rank of major in the East India Co. (which was effectively a private army tasked with exploiting the riches of the Sub-Continent for the benefit of the British Empire). In 1834, with the death of his father Hope Steuart, Major Steuart inherited Ballechin, but did not return to Scotland until 1850.

It was clear that a quarter-century spent in India had left its mark on Robert Steuart in more ways than the limp gifted by a poorly-healed leg injury. He believed in the transmigration of souls – or at least he told people that was what he believed. When the scandal blew up in June 1897 a friend of Steuart, Dr. J.A. Menzies, wrote to *The Times* describing the Major: 'I can readily believe that people who found his straightforward and uncompromising attitude in public affairs disagreeable should dislike him. Eccentric to some extent he was…. I have no doubt that he created much scandal by saying to his gardener that he had better take care to keep up the garden properly, for when he was gone his soul would go into a mole and haunt the garden and him too.' It is claimed that Robert Steuart also expressed his intention to return to this world and haunt Ballechin in the form of a black spaniel, the favourite of his many dogs. Even his friends thought of the old soldier as a bit odd, so there is no way of telling whether these were his sincere beliefs, or whether it was the estate owner's idea of a joke.

The Major seems to have largely avoided the company of his fellows, preferring to live a bachelor existence in the big house, which was run in later years by a local farmer's daughter, Sarah Nicholson. The death of the housekeeper on 14 July 1873 would later prove to be a key element in what might be called the 'Ballechin mythology'. The twenty-seven-year-old apparently suffered a short illness of three days, during which she was cared for in the master bedroom rather than the servants' quarters. So when she died, she died in the bed of sixty-eight-year-old Robert Steuart. (The bedroom is room eight on the second floor.)

In April 1876 Robert Steuart himself passed away, aged seventy-one, and was supposedly buried next to the grave of Sarah Nicholson and an unnamed Indian manservant. No monument marks the sepulchre, which is in Logierait churchyard. Under the terms of Robert Steuart's will, Ballechin was inherited by John Malcolm Skinner, the second and eldest surviving son of Robert's sister Mary. Skinner changed his surname to Steuart to ensure the continuing association of the great family's name with Ballechin. Unlike Robert, whose Oriental beliefs did not compromise his basic Protestant stance, John Skinner was a devout Roman Catholic, and made the house available to members of that faith. According to *The Alleged Haunting of B-------- House*, the new owner, who was almost forty years old when he inherited, promptly shot all his uncle's dogs. The implication was that this was accomplished to prevent the old curmudgeon's spirit from possessing the animals and thus haunting the place; it is equally possible that John Skinner was not a dog-lover and did not relish sharing a large house with fourteen hounds.

In 1880 one of Robert Steuart's surviving sisters, Isabella, died in a convent, aged sixty-six, under the name Sister Frances Helen (it was common for monks and nuns to change their names on taking religious vows). She had been a nun since 1850, the year her brother returned from India. Again, the bare facts about Isabella being a nun were destined to play a significant part in the later affair.

This, then, was the situation at the end of the 1870s. Ballechin had been the long-term home of an eccentric, solitary and crusty character who apparently believed that he could return from the dead; there had been a whiff of gossip about the younger housekeeper who died in his bed; his sister had been a nun; and the old man's nephew was a new broom who tried to sweep away as much of the old ways as possible, and opened up the house for the first time in decades to strangers, in the form of Catholic priests and nuns.

THE FIRST INCIDENTS

Reconstructing the chronology of events from published materials that turned up later, it appears the first definitely recorded incident occurred sometime between 1878 and 1880, when a Miss Yates had been the governess at Ballechin (John Skinner/Steuart had several children). In 1893 a Jesuit priest named Father Patrick Hayden had a chance meeting with the woman, who at this date kept the house for another priest. Miss Yates told Father Hayden why she had left Ballechin: 'Well, sir, so many people complained of queer noises in the house, that I got alarmed and left.' She thought she remembered that two guests – military officers – had been so disquieted by the sounds that they departed the house the next morning.

Miss Yates had not seen any strange occurrences, and appeared not to have witnessed the 'queer noises' herself, as the servants' quarters were in a small extension on the ground floor (see the plan), some distance from the epicentre of the disturbances on the second floor. This information was hugely significant for Father Hayden, for, without telling Miss Yates, he had recently had experiences of his own at Ballechin – and on the second floor.

The Jesuit had stayed at Ballechin House from 14 to 23 July 1892, during which time he tutored a group of nuns on 'retreat' in Ballechin Cottage, within the grounds of the larger house. The presence of the nuns and their instructor was part of the largesse offered to Catholics by John Skinner/Steuart. The most common incidents involved loud explosion-like sounds, or sometimes taps. Father Hayden's own account appeared in *The Alleged Haunting* book:

> I slept at B---- for nine nights, or rather one night, because I was disturbed by very queer and extraordinary noises every night except the last, which I spent in Mr S----'s [Steuart's] dressing-room. At first I occupied the room to the extreme right of the landing [No. 8], then my things were removed to another room [No. 3]… In both these rooms I heard the loud and inexplicable noises every night, but on two or three nights, in addition to these, another noise affrighted me – a sound of somebody or something falling against the door outside. It seemed, at the time, as if a calf or big dog would make such a noise. Why those particular animals came into my head I cannot tell. But in attempting to describe these indescribable phenomena, I notice now I always do say it was like a calf or big dog falling against the door. Why did I not hear the noises on the ninth night? Were there none where I was? These are questions the answers to which are not apparent. It may be there were noises, but I slept too soundly to hear them.

The Jesuit also reported that the noises seemed to be heard by no one but himself, and thought he had a vision of a brown wooden crucifix on a wall. The description of the latter came after waking and before returning to sleep, and so may have been an example of hypnagogic imagery, which can happen as you rise out of the dream state and briefly drag the dream imagery into the 'real' world. The priest mentioned his experiences to John Steuart, who suggested the sounds were caused by his late uncle, 'who was trying to attract attention in order that prayers might be offered for the repose of his soul.' Here we have a hint that there may have been some religious tension within the Steuart family: Major Steuart had been a Protestant, and in life would have looked askance at the Catholic practice of saying prayers for the dead. Was John Steuart imposing his own faith-based interpretation on the noises, or was he simply humouring the Jesuit?

Whatever the reality of the situation, Father Hayden was clearly rattled: 'It appeared to me somehow that (1) Somebody was relieved by my departure; (2) that nothing could induce me to pass another night there, at all events alone, and in other respects I do not think I am a coward.'

In opposition to these tales of strange noises, the priest himself admitted that on the night he slept soundly in John Steuart's dressing room, the 'haunted' rooms were occupied by two young female relatives of the family, and they each passed an undisturbed night. In addition, when the scandal broke, several years later, other visitors wrote to *The Times* describing the complete lack of supernatural occurrences. On 23 June 1897 Major S.F.C. Hamilton of the 4th Lancashire Fusiliers reported: 'I have slept in Ballechin, the house of my late father-in-law, hundreds of times. I have never seen or heard a ghost or had my sleep interfered with.' On the same day Mr C.L.A. Skinner wrote that he and eight members of his family, along with friends, had between them spent many nights at Ballechin since 1879, 'And not one of us has ever seen anything or heard any strange noises'. Mr Skinner also noted that when John Skinner succeeded to the property in 1876, many repairs had been needed, and that the works had somehow created 'a great deal of reverberation in the house'. And, on 21 June, Dr J.A. Menzies stated that in all the many times he had stayed at the house, he too had never heard a single hint of strange noises or of a haunted reputation.

By 1892, then, the only definitely reported unusual incidents were Miss Yates' second-hand account of scary noises, and Father Hayden's disturbed nights, which may conceivably have been down to some noises created by the nature of the house. There were no stories of apparitions, messages from beyond, or other explicit manifestations of the supernatural.

In August 1892 Father Hayden had a meeting at Falkland with John, 3rd Marquess of Bute, an extraordinary character who combined vast wealth and ownership of land and industrial concerns with mystical Catholicism and an interest in psychical research. Among his many accomplishments were the commissions of the magnificent fantasy-medieval buildings at Cardiff Castle, Castell Coch in Wales, and Mount Stuart on the Isle of Bute. In 1892 he was forty-five years old, and keenly interested in ghosts, second sight and evidence for afterlife survival. He seems to have been impressed by testimony of the thoroughly spooked Hayden, but at this date nothing more was done about Ballechin.

THE HEAVEN 'HAUNTING'

In January 1895 forty-eight-year-old John Steuart was killed in a cab accident in London. Lord Bute's supernaturally-inflected interpretation of incidents is revealed in his diary entry for the event (reproduced in *The Alleged Haunting*): 'I hear that the morning the late S---- of B---- left home for the last time, spirits came and rapped to him in his room – doubtless to warn him – so that his death was really owing to the cruel superstition which had prevented him allowing them to be communicated with.'

With the death, Ballechin passed to the next in line, John Steuart's son, army officer Captain J.M.S. Steuart. Once again a new owner brought a change in policy – out went the open-house approach to priests and nuns, and instead Ballechin and its 4,400 acres of grounds, with its fishing and shooting, were offered for medium-term lets, of the kind increasingly popular with well-heeled customers looking for a residential and sporting base in the fashionable Scottish Highlands. The first tenant was Joseph R. Heaven of Kiftsgate Court, Mickleton,

Gloucestershire. He was a naturalised Spaniard, his family name being Cielo, which means 'sky' or 'heaven'. The family, which included three sons and a daughter, took the lease for three or four months from July 1896.

The butler and two maidservants arrived on 15 July, followed three days later by two of the Heaven children, who almost immediately reported hearing strange noises at night. The butler, Harold Sanders, catalogued the incidents in a letter entitled 'On the Trail of a Ghost', published in *The Times* in June 1897. The noises were heard again over the next few nights, with the two female servants also reporting banging, rustling, footsteps, knocking and similar sounds. Sanders and some of the other young men of the family, who had now arrived, sat up through the night in a vain attempt to identify the causes of the noises. One of the watchers armed himself with a revolver. As more guests arrived the noises continued to be heard, apparently by everyone but Sanders, who considered the source to be the hot-water pipes. Eventually he was surprised out of his opinion by very loud thumping outside his door in the early hours, even though no-one was there and the service staircase and stair door restricted access to his room (the Butler Room on the ground floor, see plan).

According to Sanders, the house was in an uproar for two months:

Sometimes the whole house would be aroused. One night I remember five gentlemen meeting at the top of the stairs in their night-suits, some with sticks or pokers, one had a revolver, vowing vengeance on the disturbers of their sleep. The butler regularly kept vigil at night, and heard noises both in the main part and the wing. 'When watching I always experienced a peculiar sensation a few minutes before hearing any noise. I can only describe it as like suddenly entering an ice-house, and a feeling that some one was present and about to speak to me.' In the second week of September the phenomena apparently moved up a notch, adding physical attack to the noises: 'I had not been in bed three minutes,' wrote Sanders, 'before I experienced the sensation as before, but instead of being followed by knocking, my bedclothes were lifted up and let fall again –first at the foot of my bed, but gradually coming towards my head. I held the clothes around my neck with my hands, but they were gently lifted in spite of my efforts to hold them. I then reached around me with my hand, but could feel nothing. This was immediately followed by my being fanned as though some bird was flying around my head, and I could distinctly hear and feel something breathing on me. I then tried to reach some matches that were on a chair by my bedside, but my hand was held back as if by some invisible power. Then the thing seemed to retire to the foot of my bed. Then I suddenly found the foot of my bed lifted up and carried around towards the window for about three or four feet, then replaced to its former position.

This was still 1896, a number of months before the 'ghost-hunting' expedition and subsequent scandal of 1897. When the furore erupted that year the younger members of the Heaven family were explicitly accused of practical joking: 'One of their pranks was to drop or throw a weight upon the floor, and to draw it back by means of a string.' *(The Times, 8 June 1897)*. It was stated that the house had no previous history of haunting until the Heavens took the let, and that the pranks had directly led to the rumours, and hence the interest of the Society for Psychical Research. Joseph Heaven speedily responded, writing to the paper on 10 June that the accusations of practical joking were baseless and describing the atmosphere of the house that summer:

When I went to B---- at the beginning of August, my family had already been there a few days, and at once they told me they had found out the house was supposed to be haunted, and that they had heard most unaccountable noises. I had the greatest difficulty to persuade all my people to stay in the place, and after all, we left Scotland about the end of September, two months earlier than usual. I personally did not give any importance to the rumours that B---- House is haunted, and attributed the very remarkable noises heard to the hot-water pipes and the peculiar way in which the house is built. In fact, I have to confess I cannot believe in ghosts, and, consequently, I did my best to persuade everybody that B---- was not haunted, but I am afraid I was not always successful.

Ballechin House around 1900, three years after the SPR investigation. (*From 'The Highland Tay' by Hugh MacMillan.*)

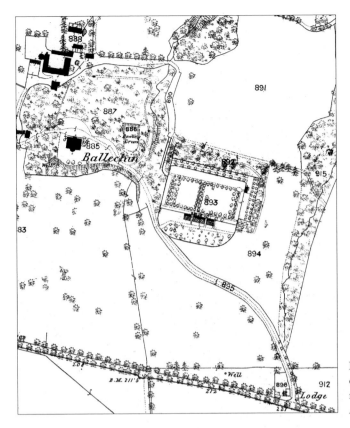

Ballechin House on the first edition of the Ordnance Survey map, in the 1860s. *(Courtesy A.K. Bell Library, Local Studies)*

Several guests who stayed at Ballechin during 1896 came forward testifying to hearing very loud knocks, bangs, groans, footsteps and other noises. None experienced visible phenomena (such as apparitions) or the physical phenomena that Harold Sanders claimed to have suffered. One visitor, Mrs Howard, published an account of her experiences in a magazine in October 1896 (and quoted extensively in *The Alleged Haunting*). As well as the strange sounds, she referred to 'a hunchback figure which is said to glide up the stairs,' 'the shadowy form of a grey lady who paces with noiseless footfall the lonely corridor' and 'a man with bronzed complexion and bent figure' who was seen passing through a solid door. A close reading of Mrs Howard's words reveals she herself did not witness any of these apparitions, and they are represented only by hearsay and standard expressions such as 'they say that…' or 'it is said that'. The single reported sighting of an apparition, that of the tanned man, has no corroborative details. The noises were so widespread and described by so many people that they were clearly objectively real; but as the only apparitions are reported by Mrs Howard, it is tempting to assume they were invented or exaggerated for the article.

This, then, was the situation at the end of 1896. The Heaven family had moved out of Ballechin early due to the 'haunting', the nature of which was disputed; members of the family, several guests, plus the staff and butler, had all reported bizarre and loud noises at night; a magazine article had been published 'bigging up' the haunting, but this did not identify Ballechin; and Captain Steuart was looking for a new short-term tenant to bring some money in.

ENTER THE SPR

The Society for Psychical Research had been founded in 1882 with the express purpose of investigating supposedly supernatural phenomena such as alleged communications with the dead (mediumship, spiritualism and so on), psychic powers (clairvoyance, telepathy, telekinesis and precognition), and similar areas such as reincarnation, poltergeists, ghosts and hauntings. From the beginning it prided itself as an organisation dedicated to a scientific and rational interrogation of the realm of the paranormal, and is still actively pursuing these aims. Its extensive files are a treasure trove for researchers.

By December 1896 the SPR had decided that Ballechin would provide an ideal subject for a new kind of 'long-form' experiment. The house was to be rented for several months, with a SPR member as the co-ordinator; and various guests invited to stay, some linked to the SPR and psychic research, and some not at all interested in the subject. If the house was genuinely haunted it was hoped that various people would observe the phenomena, and their corresponding testimonies provide verification of the haunting. The costs of renting Ballechin, including the wages of the servants, were borne by Lord Bute.

And so began what has become the template for dozens of fictional ghost stories and horror films: put a disparate group of people in a large, allegedly haunted mansion, and await developments of the spooky kind.

Theoretically the proceedings could have been very productive from the point of view of psychical research – but only, of course, if the reports of previous hauntings were indeed reliable, which is not certain, and, indeed, only if the people at the centre of the investigation were paragons of probity.

The person chosen by the SPR as the resident organiser at Ballechin was Ada Goodrich Freer. She was energetic, vivacious and possessed of great charm and a capacity for hard work. From 1892 she had been working on the Society's Enquiry into Second Sight in the Highlands, an activity for which she lacked one key skill (a knowledge of Gaelic) while possessing another ability in abundance (the tendency to exaggerate the value of her findings and mislead her sponsors). As a result the Enquiry did not generate any useful results.

A fascinating, complex character, Miss Freer could be described as a liminal person, that is, someone who walked the borders between different human worlds, disguising who and what she was. She was an active member of the scientifically-minded Society for Psychical Research, yet was also the assistant editor of the Spiritualist periodical *Borderland* (which was sometimes at loggerheads with the SPR). Further, she was a practicing clairvoyant professing 'sensitive' gifts, automatic writing ability under trance, crystal vision (seeing things in crystal balls) and shell hearing (the ability to receive paranormal communications through seashells). She could just as easily have been a subject for investigation rather than an investigator. Her penname for articles was 'Miss X'.

She had also renegotiated class boundaries – or, more exactly, had simply chosen to manipulate them to her own advantage. Of middling origins and usually short of cash, she routinely lied about her relatively humble background and happily pretended to be upper middle class so as to successfully fit in with the well-heeled ladies and gentlemen of the Society. Further, she had the good fortune to look far younger than she actually was, and throughout her life consistently subtracted ten or fifteen years from her actual age without anyone knowing.

This tendency to be economical with the *actualité* also informed her professional life, so she could take the work of others and pass it off as her own, or downplay or exaggerate elements as she pleased. In some ways her combination of intellect, drive, ruthlessness and tendency to manipulate the truth to her own benefit, all packaged in the seemingly harmless form of an attractive and respectable lady of means, makes her a kind of trickster figure, a character who challenges and subverts conventions in many folklore tales.

Ballechin was leased in the name of SPR member Colonel Lemesurier Taylor, who claimed to be looking for a sporting vacation for himself and his family. In point of pact, the Colonel was a widower, had no family, and had no interest in fishing or shooting. The ghost investigation was never mentioned to Captain Steuart or his representatives (when the scandal erupted, this subterfuge caused considerable embarrassment to the SPR and great annoyance to the Steuarts). Miss Freer engaged the servants and, on 3 February 1897, took up residence at Ballechin.

Over the next few months what was effectively a psychological as well as a para-psychological experiment was conducted with the walls of the grand house – some visitors, intent merely on the joys of country house living and being toffs on a Highland estate, had no idea they had come to a 'haunted house' until they arrived. Around thirty-five to forty ladies and gentlemen came as guests, some staying for a few days, others remaining longer. They included men of the cloth, military officers, academics, lawyers, doctors, businessmen, students, 'sensitives' and mediums, and a peer of the realm (Lord Bute). Invitation to stay seems to have been *ad hoc*, with some guests suggested because they were scientists or otherwise useful to the investigation, while others came along simply because they were friends of friends. Among the visitors were Professor Oliver Lodge, the Honorable Everard Feilding, Sir James Crichton-Browne, Father Allan McDonald, Archbishop Angus McDonald of St Andrews and Edinburgh, Revd Charles J.M. Shaw, the author Andrew Lang, Mr (later Sir) John Ritchie Findlay (son and heir of the owner of the *Scotsman*) and F.W.H. Myers, one of the founders of the SPR.

A PANOPLY OF PHANTOMS

The noises did not disappoint, and soon there were multiple reports of clangs, sounds like gunshots or explosions, draggings, footsteps and voices – including what was interpreted as the sound of a priest reading aloud the Catholic daily service. Rooms 1, 3 and 8 were especially favoured with anomalous acoustic events, some extremely loud. Miss Freer, who was the effective manager of the experiment, responsible for everything from organising the allocation of rooms to keeping a journal of events, operated a Ouija board, producing the names Margaret and Ishbel, which some present related to Isabella Margaret, the two first names of the sister of Major Steuart. The Ouija board seemed to have been used on a nightly basis, and sometimes gave 'instructions' as to when and where some kind of phenomenon would manifest.

At some point Miss Freer added what might be called an 'explanatory narrative'. New guests were regaled with her description of the 'wicked major' Robert Steuart, alongside his peccadilloes, and the stories of the dogs, the death of the housekeeper, and the subsequent history of religious visitors. This narrative, delivered with great skill during evening gatherings in the drawing room, seemed to influence the interpretation of subsequent events, and some members of the party became convinced Major Steuart, Sarah Nicholson, and even the nuns, were still in the building. In other words, the interpretation of the phenomena was heavily influenced by the power of suggestion, and as such the investigation was fatally flawed from the moment Miss Freer started telling her ghost stories in the drawing room (some would argue the entire operation was compromised as soon as communications via the Ouija board started to be taken seriously and allowed to influence the guests' behaviour).

The noises were the one constant, although the interpretation of what they meant depended on the individual. Colonel Taylor, who was disappointed in his hope of experiencing some kind of genuine supernatural event during his five weeks' residence, thought they were similar to sounds he had heard in other country houses, and concluded they had a prosaic source. Revd Shaw, who according to John Ritchie Findlay had an apparently uncritical devotion to the paranormal hypothesis, was convinced the sounds were both supernatural and sentient.

Apparitions now started arriving with increasing frequency. On several occasions Miss Freer saw a black-clad nun and a woman in grey within the grounds; most of the time her companions saw nothing, although a young sensitive named Miss Langton, plus the aforementioned Revd Shaw, thought they saw something similar on one occasion. Miss Langton later woke in room 2 – supposedly a quiet room – to see the figure of a nun form as if out of mist, become solid for a few minutes, and then vanish. The sensitive had also had an earlier sighting of a phantom she later recognised as the double of Father Hayden when she met him in a railway station. Revd Shaw also had a brief vision of brown wooden crucifix in room 3. Carter, the upper housemaid, woke in the early hours to see an old woman at the foot of her bed. Miss Freer saw a solid-looking old female servant enter the drawing room and then vanish, and spotted a small and very real-looking black spaniel (which was thought to be significant as Major Steuart's favourite dog had been a spaniel, and the sighting occurred on the anniversary of the Major's death). Later Miss Freer saw 'two black paws resting on the table beside the bed'. Another medium became aware of the 'shadowy figure of an old man' in a darkened corridor.

OTHER PHENOMENA

The 23-25 March brought an escalation in the physical and other phenomena. Another psychic, Miss Fyfe (given the pseudonym Duff), described her experience:

> I was awakened as if by someone violently shaking my bed… and at the same time I felt something press heavily upon me… it was not at all such a vibration as might be caused by a high wind or any ordinary movement occurring in other parts of the House. The bed seemed to heave in the centre, as if there were some force under it, which raised it in the centre and rocked it violently for a moment and then let it sink again… The highest point on the 'Switchback' [a rollercoaster] is the nearest to it in my experience. I was wide awake at the time, so it was no nightmare.

The following night Lizzie, the kitchenmaid, had some kind of vision or hallucination of 'a cloud which changed rapidly in colour, shape, and size, and alarmed her greatly' and then felt her bedclothes pulled off. Her screams brought the other maids, who spent the rest of the night in the housemaid's room and thereafter all slept in the one room. And the next night, Miss Fyfe again felt her bed shake. On other dates both Miss Freer and Miss Langton felt a push, as if they had been nudged by a dog seeking attention; at other times various guests complained of 'chills' or a sense of presence.

THE END GAME

From the middle of April several guests described a feeling of hostility, malevolence or even evil pervading the house. So bad did this become that it was decided to have the house blessed by a Roman Catholic bishop. Archbishop Angus McDonald arrived, preceded by Father Allan McDonald and another priest who during their stay were, according to Miss Freer, both convinced dark forces were at work. Mass was said, attended by all the Catholics amongst the staff and visitors, and then the archbishop and the priests processed around the house, blessing each room in turn with holy water. Especial attention was paid to rooms 1, 3, and 8, the library, and the doorway to the drawing-room – all hotspots for noises and other phenomena.

Following the blessing the noises reduced in intensity and no further apparitions were seen. The first part of May saw several new visitors, who experienced nothing very untoward. By 13 May the tenancy was completed. An extraordinary three months had come to an end.

THE ERUPTION

One of the guests who visited during the quiet end of the tenancy was a lead writer for *The Times*, J. Callender Ross. On 8 June he penned for the newspaper an extended and anonymous attack on the Ballechin investigation, castigating the Society for Psychical Research, and implicitly criticising Miss Freer as an amateur whose gender and role as a hostess made her unsuited to lead such an investigation. The whole episode was regarded as a sham – Ballechin had never had a haunted reputation, the article claimed, and Lord Bute had effectively been sold a pup:

> It was represented to him [Lord Bute] that he was taking 'the most haunted house in Scotland',
> a house with an old and established reputation for mysteries if not supernatural disturbances.
> What he has got is a house with no reputation whatever of that kind, with no history, with
> nothing germane to his purpose beyond a cloud of baseless rumours produced during the last
> twelve months.

Further, the Steuarts had been misled as to the exact nature of the lease, and the stories of ghosts would adversely affect the price of the house (if there was one thing that got the readers of 'The Thunderer' incensed, it was an attack on the sacred value of property).

Over the following days the letters columns of the top people's paper were ablaze with indignation, accusation and counter-accusation. The case of Ballechin House, which might have provided acres of material for the SPR to analyse had it gone unnoticed by the wider world, suddenly became an embarrassment for the Society. Faced with intense criticism by their peers, the SPR closed ranks, denied any official involvement in the experiment – and threw Ada Goodrich Freer to the wolves. F.W.H. Myers, who had stayed at Ballechin for ten days and had previously been very enthusiastic about the investigation and Miss Freer's interim reports, quickly wrote to *The Times*, the letter appearing on 10 June:

> SIR,--A letter entitled 'On the Trail of a Ghost,' which you publish to-day, appears to suggest throughout that some statement has been made on behalf of the Society for Psychical Research with regard to the house which your correspondent visited. This, however, is not the case; and as a misleading impression may be created, I must ask you to allow me space to state that I visited B----, representing that society, before your correspondent's visit, and decided that there was no such evidence as could justify us in giving the results of the inquiry a place in our *Proceedings*. I had already communicated this judgment to Lord Bute, to the council of the society, and to Professor Sidgwick, the editor of our Proceedings, and it had been agreed to act upon it.
> I am, Sir, your obedient servant,
> FREDERICK W.H. MYERS,
> Hon. Sec. of the Society for Psychical Research.

A further and more direct disclaimer appeared in the *Journal of the Society for Psychical Research*:

> There is still an impression in certain quarters that the Society is responsible for the hiring of Ballechin House, with a view to the investigation of phenomena alleged to occur there. The Council therefore desire to make it known to all readers of the *Journal* that this impression is altogether erroneous. The question of hiring Ballechin House was never brought before the Council in any form whatever, and they are entirely without responsibility with regard to it.

Irrespective of the quality of the results at Ballechin, this was a shabby response. The SPR had been directly behind the lease of the house, the employment of Miss Freer, and the intended nature of the 'long term' investigation. Indeed, correspondence published in *The Alleged Haunting of B------- House* and Campbell and Hall's investigative book *Strange Things* clearly sets out the extent to which senior members of the Society were committed to the investigation. But the situation demanded a sacrifice, and Miss Freer was the chosen victim.

THE AFTERMATH

Despite the voluminous documentary material, no analysis of the reported phenomena at Ballechin appeared in the pages of the SPR's *Journal* or *Proceedings*. The relationship between Miss Freer and the SPR was poisoned for ever. In 1899, two years after the controversy, she published, with Lord Bute as her co-author, *The Alleged Haunting of B------- House*. Although the names of Ballechin and some of the key players in the drama had been well ventilated in the press, the book retained the convention of referring to places and people only by initials or through pseudonyms. A second edition came out in 1900, the year Lord Bute died. With her principal patron gone, Miss Freer moved out of psychical research and into folklore, extensively plagiarising the notes gathered in the Hebrides by Father Allan MacDonald (one of the guests at Ballechin), and publishing them under her own name.

WHAT REALLY HAPPENED AT BALLECHIN?

The controversy in *The Times* and the subsequent distancing of the SPR from the investigation has blighted all subsequent attempts at understanding what when on there during the two separate extensive hauntings of 1896 and 1897. An analysis of the phenomena shows that strange, loud sounds of various kinds were reported by a majority of guests and staff. There is thus no difficulty in stating that these noises were objectively real. But what caused them? Several ingenious suggestions have been put forward for physical origins, from noises caused by earth tremors or rock faulting, to the breaking up of ice in unsuspected underground channels. Initially this latter hypothesis seems attractive, as in 1897 the noises did cease once the warmer weather kicked in; however, noises were heard right throughout the hottest months in 1896. The peculiarities of the plumbing system in the house were often commented on by sceptical visitors, while there may have been something in the fabric of the building that responded noisily to the wind or changes in temperature or pressure.

Another possibility is human agency, with some parties possibly engaged in pranks for their own ends. Against this notion is that the two episodes – the Heaven haunting of 1896 and the SPR haunting of 1897 – had no persons in common, either in visitors or staff. Of course, this does not mean that, once the notion of the 'haunted house' had been established, someone decided to help things along a bit. *Strange Things* published a letter from Professor

Ballechin House shortly before its demolition in 1963. *(Crown Copyright: RCAHMS. Licensor www.rcahms.gov.uk)*

W. A. F. Balfour-Browne, who as a young man of twenty-three had visited Ballechin towards the end of the SPR tenancy. He revealed that he had found and crawled through a small passage that ran through the top floor. In his opinion someone could have 'played ghosts' while hidden in this passage. On the other hand, with the exception of one episode when some noises outside were connected to a probable poacher, there was no evidence ever implicating anyone in noise-making during the SPR tenancy. The Heaven occupation may be a different matter, and despite the fervent denials of practical joking by the family, suspicions linger that some of the high-spirited younger members may have contributed to the events. We will never know.

Somewhat less likely is the suggestion argued by the Honourable John Harris in his book *Inferences from Haunted Houses and Haunted Men*, published in 1901. Harris appears to have been obsessed with the idea of criminal gangs of hypnotists, who he regarded as responsible for many reports of haunted houses. The book breathes a deep paranoia from every page. In exhaustive detail, Harris shows how every reported incident from Ballechin was created by one such gang for their own nefarious purposes; the 'nuns' seen by Miss Freer were in fact the very hypnotists making their way through the grounds.

When it comes to the apparitions, several commentators have noticed that most were reported by Miss Freer. Private letters and reminiscences published in *Strange Things* demonstrate that some guests noted Miss Freer's capacity for exaggeration when compared to the accounts of other witnesses. She has been shown to have had a strong tendency to manipulate and invent facts in other contexts. The authors of *Strange Things* wonder if Miss Freer's powerful personality had imposed itself on other less robust individuals, leading to the power of suggestion and the development of 'group think'. If this was the case, some or many of the incidents reported by the other witnesses may be suspect. Once again, we will almost certainly never know what really happened, but on the balance of probabilities there are grounds not to believe everything that Miss Freer wrote down in *The Alleged Haunting*.

The final possibility is that at least some of the incidents during the SPR tenancy had a genuine preternatural quality. Alas, the truth or otherwise of this will always elude us, because Ballechin House is no more.

THE LAST RITES

In 1932 the property was sold by the Steuart family to Mr Wemyss Honeyman. After his death Ballechin was left uninhabited and became riddled with dry rot. Eventually it became a lost cause and was demolished to the very foundations in 1963. The grounds are private and there is no access. And so now nothing remains of what, even if it was not 'the most haunted house in Scotland', was the epicentre of a truly bizarre, truly intriguing, and truly scandalous late Victorian horror-show. Strange things, indeed.

FOUR

MAGGIE WALL – THE WITCH WHO NEVER WAS

'It is a riddle, wrapped in a mystery, inside an enigma; but perhaps there is a key.'
Winston Churchill discussing Russia in a radio broadcast, October 1939.

It stands, gaunt and alone, on the roadside west of the Strathearn village of Dunning. A tall, spindly, grey cross, mounted atop a cairn of substantial boulders, some of them bounded by iron clasps. Daubed in white paint on the upper stones are the words:

Maggie Wall
burnt here
1657 as a Witch

The Maggie Wall Monument is the only historic monument to a named witch in the whole of Britain. Its story has baffled successive generations of visitors and residents. The key unanswered questions are:

Who was Maggie Wall?
Why, of all the witches in the country, does she have a personalised monument?
When was the monument built?
Who built it, and why?
And who mysteriously renews the paint on a regular basis?

Now, for the first time, some of these questions can be answered.

A LITTLE BACKGROUND

The monument's earliest appearance in the public record is on the first edition of the Ordnance Survey map, surveyed in 1863-64 and based on the list of placenames compiled by the OS for their *Name Book* in 1859. The map shows the monument and states that it bears the legend 'Maggie Walls Burned here for Witchcraft 1657', which is slightly different to the inscription as it reads now. Either this was not a literal transcription or the wording has changed over time. The Ordnance Survey map also shows that the trees then surrounding the monument were known as Maggie Walls Wood. And – at least until now – the monument stands in a sea of mystery, absent from any document before 1859, missing from memoirs and official records alike: its purpose, date of erection and origin remain unknown. Added to this is the strange fact that Maggie Wall herself is completely unknown to history.

The enigmatic Maggie Wall Monument near Dunning. *(Photo by Geoff Holder)*

The painted words on the cairn. One of the blasting holes can be seen between the '16' and '57'. *(Photo by Geoff Holder)*

WITCH MONUMENT, DUNNING.

Left: The Monument sometime between 1900 and 1910. Note the style of the painted words has changed slightly since, and that the site was once surrounded by trees. *(AK Bell Library, Local Studies)*

Below: The Monument and Maggie Walls Wood, recorded on the first edition of the Ordnance Survey map in 1863. *(Courtesy A.K. Bell Library, Local Studies)*

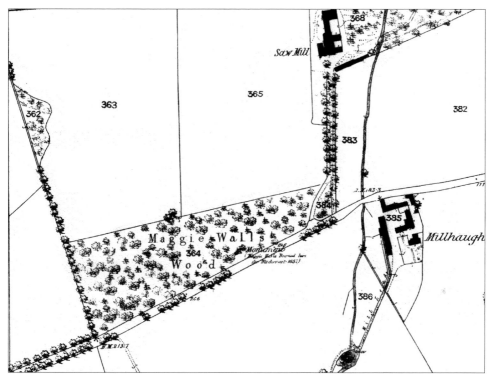

THE DUNNING WITCHES

From 1563 a 'guilty' verdict of witchcraft meant a death sentence, a situation that remained until the law was changed in 1735. Strathearn was no stranger to witches and witch trials in the seventeenth century. In May 1662 the Privy Council, the supreme legal institution in Scotland at the time, issued several Commissions of Justiciary to local gentlemen in the area. This was standard practice at the time – the Privy Council, unable to deal with witchcraft cases far from its base in Edinburgh, effectively delegated the administration of justice to the local gentry on a temporary, case-by-case basis. Usually a Commission was issued when strong evidence had been found to suggest an individual or a group were guilty of witchcraft. Typically this evidence had been supplied by a local minister keen on rooting out witchcraft in his parish. However, as witchcraft was a capital crime, the Church had no authority to conduct the trial, and had to hand the process over to the civic authorities. For lesser crimes, such as 'charming' or folk magic, the church had the legal power to act because the penalties were less severe. So, for instance, the Synod of the Church of Scotland came to Dunning in 1657 to censure a charmer named Johnnie Guthrie; punished with excommunication, Guthrie does not feature in the records thereafter.

So in 1662 around ten members of the prominent Strathearn families the Oliphants, Hays, Moncreiffs, Drummonds and Rollos assembled to put seventeen women on trial for their lives. Unfortunately the details of the accusations and the processes of the trials have been lost, but we do know all the women had been imprisoned, and that none of them confessed, a telling fact which suggests torture (which was legal) had not been used. We also know the names of these 'witches', and we know what happened to them. The trials commenced on 7 May, and on 28 July a second Commission was issued to pronounce and put into effect the death sentence on eight women who had been found guilty.

Issobell McKendley, Elspeth Reid and Jonet Toyes of Dunning, Jonet Airth of Pothill of Aberuthven, Helen Ilson and Margret Crose of Forteviot, Jonet Martin of Nethergask at Findo Gask and Jonet Young of Clathimore at Findo Gask were all strangled to death and then burned, the standard fate for convicted Scottish witches. Nine other accused – Jonet Bining and Agnes Ramsey of Clathimore at Findo Gask, Jonet Allan of Overgask at Findo Gask, Jonet Robe at Woodhead of Findo Gask, Jonnet Annand and Elizabeth Clow of Forgan, and Issobell Goold, Agnes Hutsone and Anna Law, all of Dunning – vanish from the records and were presumably released. The traditional site for the executions has for centuries been regarded as nearby Kincladie Wood.

Of the women executed, we know the most about Issobell McKendley of Dunning. In 1658 she clearly had something of a local reputation as a healer, for she turns up in a two-year-long church investigation into charming that lasted until 1660. When Margaret Dick from Kintillo was examined by the Dunbarney Kirk Session, she confessed to hiring Issobell to cure her daughter-in-law Janet Imrie, and doing the same for her own daughter Christian Scot two years previously. She also knew that several other women had employed Issobell, who was typically paid with barley or peas. The Dunning healer clearly employed sympathetic magic, transferring the illness from the sufferers into inanimate objects such as clods of earth or stones; when someone else accidentally touched these charged items, the sickness was transmitted to them, which completed the original cure. For her pains Issobell was reported to the

Auchterarder Presbytery. No doubt this decade-long reputation as a 'wise woman' formed part of her accusations in 1662.

But the name Maggie Wall, Maggie Walls or anything similar appears nowhere in the witch trials of 1662, nor does it feature in the parish records, or indeed anywhere in the entire vast corpus of Scottish witchcraft archives. The nearest equivalent names are Margaret Wallace, executed in Glasgow on 20 March 1622; two other women of the same name accused in Langton and Ayr in 1629, their fate not being recorded; and a person of unknown gender named 'Wallace' or 'Wallas', who appears in the records for Ayr in 1658, fate unknown. As far as the documentary record goes, Maggie never existed.

THE FOLKLORE

I have lost count of the number of people who have told me that Maggie Wall was a healer, or a seer, or a wise woman, and that she had been put to death on a trumped-up charge of witchcraft by a vengeful and intolerant Church. Unfortunately, no one could take the story back further than it was 'what their parents had told them', and no details are ever available as to who did the burning, or when the monument was put up. Sadly there is no authentic tradition attached to Maggie, and all the tales have a generic quality about them that suggests the stories were made up to explain the presence of the monument, rather than the stories preceding the monument.

One interesting variation on the standard version was passed to me by long-term village resident David Doig. As a boy he was told Maggie was a maid at the old castle of Duncrub; when she became pregnant by the laird's son the Rollo family decided to dispose of the problem by accusing her of witchcraft and having her burned. Interesting though this variant is, it still conforms to a well-known folkloric narrative, that of wicked aristocrats seducing and then abandoning or murdering lower-class women. It also ignores one of the key obstacles to all the 'unrecorded execution' tales: witchcraft trials in Scotland were a legalistic process, involving judges, prosecutors, witnesses, confessions, and due legal process. The nature of this process becomes clear when you realise how many people were accused of witchcraft yet released for lack of evidence (for example, nine out of the seventeen accused at Dunning were released, because under the law the evidence was not strong enough to support a conviction). This was not mob rule, nor could powerful individuals easily take the law into their own hands. Burning witches without a Commission from the Privy Council was quite simply murder. While Commissioned individuals sometimes bent the law to go further than their remit allowed (as at nearby Rhynd in 1662, when the minister and his bigoted cronies used their Commission for a few named witches as an excuse to go after all witches), there is no record of any single, spontaneous act of illegal witch-murder anywhere in Scotland during the period 1563-1735, the years when witchcraft was punishable by death.

THE ARCHAEOLOGY

It is sometimes said that the monument was erected by people who remembered Maggie from their own lifetimes, placing the construction in the late seventeenth century. But this cannot be,

Above: One of the several date-diagnostic blasting holes on the border of the cairn. The candle is one of many ritual items left at the monument. *(Photo by Geoff Holder)*

Left: Another item on the cairn, this one Hallowe'en-related. *(Photo by Geoff Holder)*

as the physical evidence shows. In 2004 archaeologist David Connolly surveyed the monument on behalf of the BBC Radio Scotland programme *Past Lives*, and in 2010 he kindly passed his findings on to me in a personal communication. The key finding was that the cross-shaft is a re-used eighteenth century lintel, as shown by the toolmarks distinctive to the period; when the lintel was removed from its previous building the cross was carved out of one end. Unfortunately the marks are not sufficiently diagnostic to give a date other than some time in the 1700s.

The second area of interest is the drill holes that are easily visible on several boulders in the cairn. These holes are characteristic of quarry blasting, being drilled for the insertion of gunpowder. Blasting using this technique typically indicates a nineteenth-century date. However, as David pointed out, a French work (the *Encyclopedie of Diderot & D'Alembert*) shows iron-ore miners were drilling blasting holes in the 1760s, and the technique was known in America by the late 1790s. So it is possible the drilling took place in the last decades of the eighteenth century or the first years of the 1800s.

What this analysis clearly shows, by the way, is something which is obvious to anyone who studies the monument – this took a lot of work. The cairn was not built in an afternoon – the boulders had to be quarried using gunpowder, transported to this spot, and then erected around the re-carved lintel. Whoever put the monument up had done their planning and had access to both human resources and the raw materials. Whoever did it was a person of determination and substance. So why had they gone to all this trouble to commemorate a witch?

WHO WAS MAGGIE WALL? THE AWFUL TRUTH

Since at least the 1870s, when John Wilson, the local minister, combed the parish records and came up empty, it has been assumed that Maggie had been a real person whose name somehow had been missing in the official records. She must have been existed, the argument went, or else why was the monument erected? The lack of documentation was irrelevant: the monument existed, and therefore so had Maggie.

But this is not true. For Maggie Wall never existed.

The proof is in a large wall-sized map of the Duncrub Estate, the home turf of the wealthy Rollo family, land magnates in the Dunning area. Although it is in private hands, the map has been catalogued by the National Archives of Scotland and is titled, 'A Plan of the Lordship of [?] Humbly [?] to the Rt. Hon. Robert Lord Rollo by ? William Winter'. The question marks represent the damage to the map's title, but the remainder of the document is in excellent condition. It is essentially a plan designed for business management, as it includes careful drawings of all the fields and properties on the estate, and lists their acreages, crop yields, quality of soil, and so on.

The truth revealed: the field-name 'Maggie's walls' on an estate plan of 1755. *(Photo by Geoff Holder)*

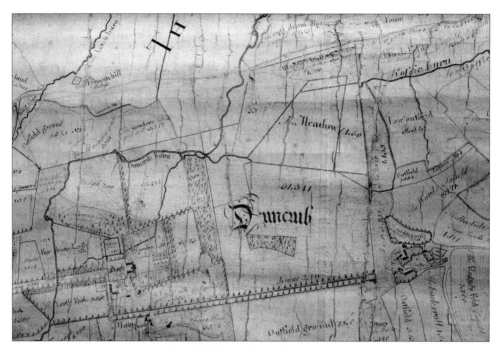

The estate map of 1755. North is at the bottom. Duncrub House is lower left, the enclosed field called Maggie's walls is at the top, above The Meadow. *(Photo by Geoff Holder)*

Initially the plan is confusingly eccentric by modern standards, as south is to the top, and so the standard way of reading a map has to be inverted. But the writing is clear, its ink still largely unfaded after more than 250 years. For the plan is dated 1755. And near the centre is a field named Maggie's walls.

Not Maggie Wall or Maggie Walls, but Maggie's walls, 'as being ground from the meadow, light Soil.' It is a placename, referring to a walled field, and the linear, almost right-angled walls can clearly be seen. Who Maggie was is unknown, but her surname was not Walls. Because the name refers to the stone dyke that still encloses the field. The field called Maggie's walls. A placename that was later borrowed and applied to a monument to someone who could not have existed.

The walls can even be dated, for at the western end of the dyke running alongside the road in front of the monument, are three inscribed stones. One reads 'DUNCRUB', another 'H R BUILT THIS PARK 1722'. 'H R' was the Honorable Henry Rollo, second son of Robert, the 4th Lord Rollo. Born in 1705, Henry was married not long after his nineteenth birthday and appears to have devoted his youthful energies to improving the estate while his elder brother Andrew (later the 5th Lord Rollo) was away elsewhere. (A puzzle is that the third inscribed stone appears to read '18 4 H1' or 'IB 4 HI'. I have no idea what this means).

WHEN WAS THE MONUMENT BUILT?

So, the wall around the field was built in 1722, and the name Maggie's walls is first recorded in 1755. The monument dedicated to Maggie Wall the witch first appears on record in 1859.

One of inscribed stones on the dyke enclosing the field: 'H R BULT THIS PARK 1722'. H R was Henry Rollo. *(Photo by Geoff Holder)*

This inscribed stone is close to the one above. Does it read '18 4 H1' or 'IB 4 HI'? *(Photo by Geoff Holder)*

We have roughly a hundred years in which to locate the construction. I am inclined to dismiss a late date because when the Revd John Wilson was writing his book *Dunning: Its Parochial History* in 1873, none of the inhabitants of the village could contribute anything useful about the monument, implying its erection had already passed out of living memory. The toolmarks, blast holes and other archaeological evidence suggest a date of the late eighteenth or early nineteenth century.

WHO BUILT THE MONUMENT?

The following paragraphs are speculation based on the known facts, as listed above, and combined with my best guess as to the likely candidate for the builder. Whoever did it obviously could command skilled labour and quarried stone, seemed to have a surplus lintel from an old building to hand, and also had access to the field of Maggie's walls. I also reasoned that they were educated and had some knowledge of local history, as it's possible the monument refers to some forgotten incident the builder thought was important.

The Duncrub Estate Factors' Book for 1797: 'Rent of Muggies walls possessed by Adam Moodie and David Balmain, 1797, £2 10s'. (*The National Archives of Scotland*)

The Duncrub accounts for 1799: 'Rents of Muggies walls Crop 1799. Possessed by Mr Balmain for which he says he accounted by Coals furnished the Soldiers during Militia Riots – £2 10s' (*The National Archives of Scotland*)

One individual fits the criteria: David Balmain, the village schoolmaster.

Mr Balmain clearly was a lad o' parts, with fingers in many pies. The National Archives of Scotland hold an extensive collection of historic papers relating to the Duncrub estate, among them a ragtaggle collection of household and factors' accounts, land rentals, letters, ledgers and cash books, all bound in leather and filled with beautifully-composed but hard-to-read eighteenth-century copperplate handwriting. Deep within this dusty treasure trove, David Balmain starts to appear from 1780, first as the writer of feu records (the documents setting out the rental of land from the feudal superior, Lord Rollo). Presumably he got the job because he was one of the few educated and literate people in the district. In 1794 he was joint tenant of the farm Thainsland with John Baine. By 1795 he was tenant of the farms Pitmeadows and Trees, and being granted 230 bolls of lime to repair the walls and farm buildings left in a state of disrepair by the previous tenant. He was also drawing a schoolmaster's salary of £4 13s 7¾d, and over two years had been paid two large sums, £20 0s 2d and £30, to build a new manse and barn. In 1796 his salary had risen to £5 12s 4½d and he received a further emolument of £15 0s 2d to continue working on the manse. The same year he was granted another boon of lime to upgrade his farm buildings, and the account books at this time are filled with mentions of improvements and repairs elsewhere on the estate. In January 1797 another £20 made his way 'to account of new manse'. There are several other mentions of him paying rents on at least two properties.

Mr Balmain's little empire was clearly doing quite nicely, and he expanded further. In 1797 we see the first mention of his tenancy of a new strip of land – called Muggies walls. He is shown as a joint tenant with Adam Moodie, who in 1794 was described as a butcher in Dunning. Between them they paid an annual rent of £2 10s for the field. By 1799 Mr Moodie was no longer on the joint tenancy, and Mr Balmain was avoiding paying his rent on the field: 'Whereas the following arrears are irrecoverable… Rents of Muggies Walls Crop 1799. Professed by Mr Balmain for which he says he accounted by Coals furnished the Soldiers during militia riots £2 10s.'

So we have an educated and energetic local man doing quite nicely from his salary and his various projects. He is renovating a farmhouse and a manse, so he may well have the odd stone lintel to hand. He is engaged in substantial building works, and therefore has access to workmen, raw materials, quarried stone, and other elements useful in building a substantial monument. And, crucially, he is the tenant of the field called Maggie's or Muggies walls in the late 1790s, which fits in with the archaeological evidence.

I therefore propose David Balmain as the man most likely to have built the Maggie Wall Monument. Sadly I have been unable to uncover any document that directly links man and monument, so the connection is ultimately unproven.

WHY WAS THE MONUMENT BUILT?

Archaeology and raw financial documents can rarely provide us with an insight into the emotions and motivations of the people concerned, and there is nothing to even hint as to why the village schoolmaster and building entrepreneur should decide to build a monument to a witch who did not exist.

Several possibilities suggest themselves, some of which are more speculative than others:

The first possibility is that David Balmain had fallen under the spell of Walter Scott, the hugely successful novelist who was single-handedly responsible for reimagining Scotland in a new romantic light. Scott reworked Scottish history, often inventing episodes which later became to be regarded as 'true'. Historians have been struggling to disentangle fact from Scott's fantasy ever since (archaeologist David Connolly told me he would like to go back in a time machine 'and give Scott a slap'). Scott's well-heeled fans often 'romanticised' their estates in imitation, building follies and adding faux historical features, even inventing 'traditions'. Scott's influence first took off in the first decade of the nineteenth century, and it is known he spent some time travelling in Perthshire. The account books for 1806-1814 are either missing or incomplete, so we cannot see if David Balmain was still the tenant of Maggie's walls in that time, but it is possible, and therefore he might have taken Scott's influence and looked at his local history, creating both a romantic legend and a romantic folly.

Another consideration is that Balmain was making a reference to an actual event from 1657. In that year the Presbytery of the Church of Scotland visited Dunning to investigate the minister, Andrew Rollo. Andrew was the fourth son of the 1st Lord Rollo, and held the charge at Dunning from 1652 to 1668. He had changed his spots each time the religious complexion of seventeenth-century Scotland altered, and at various times had been an enthusiastic Episcopalian, Covenanter, Presbyterian supporter of Cromwell, and finally an Episcopalian again. The records are vague to the point of being useless, but he was gravely warned to 'be circumspect in his carriage for times to come' and to keep out of alehouses and similar bad places on the Lord's Day. Could there have been some kind of scandal involving a woman? It is impossible to tell.

The third speculative idea brings us back to witches again. James, 2nd Lord Rollo (1600-1669), had been on the Commissions that had condemned eight women to death in 1662. Also on the Commission was his slightly younger brother the Honorable Laurence Rollo of Rossie, the third son of the 1st Lord Rollo. Was Balmain reflecting some kind of local grudge against the local toffs, or was he trying to prick the conscience of the Rollos? Was the monument a cenotaph to all the witches executed at Dunning, with 'Maggie Wall' a composite figure whose name he simply borrowed from the field where he chose to place his memorial? Could it even have been a subtle dig at the Rollos, despite them bankrolling his projects? Had he fallen out with the Rollos in some way?

My fourth suggestion is truly out on a limb. In 1657 Issobell McKendley was called in to cure Margaret Imrie's husband in Kintillo, whose name is given as Ninian Balman. The healer told a woman named Bessie Belmain to wash Ninian's shirt and pass a live chicken through the garment. The illness transferred from the shirt to the chicken, and when Ninian donned the sark again, he was cured, a classic case of sympathetic magic. Issobell McKendley was one of the eight witches executed in 1662. Could Ninian Balman and Bessie Belmain have been ancestral relations of David Balmain? Was there a family story about the cure? And in constructing the monument, was the schoolmaster somehow honouring a woman who had helped his ancestor, and was later executed? Like I say, it's out on a limb.

I am certain readers can come up with their own ideas about why David Balmain did such a thing. Perhaps we will never know.

THE PAINTED WORDS

If you compare the two photographs, one dating from 2010 and the other from over a hundred years earlier, you can see that the style of the painted letters has changed ever so slightly over time. This is an effect of the multiple repaintings over the years. The identity of those responsible has been as much a mystery as any other aspect of the monument, and clearly it has been undertaken by several generations of anonymous caretakers. Through local enquiries I am reasonably certain the most recent contributor was the late Mrs Sanderson, who lived at Keltie Castle almost opposite the monument. After she died the task has been adopted by another long-term resident of the village, who told me he last applied the paint in around 2007 or 2008.

SOME FEATURES OF THE MONUMENT AND LANDSCAPE

In the post-war years Duncrub Estate was sold and broken up. Along with much of the woodland, Maggie Walls Wood was cut down and sold as timber; as it has not been replanted, the open space has been known as Maggie Walls Field since then. The loss of the trees makes the monument starker, even, in some circumstances, slightly menacing. Up until 1964 there was no entrance through the dyke and visitors were climbing over the wall and damaging the stones. That year, as David Doig told me,

The rear of the cross, showing the repairs made after the vandalism in 1998. *(Photo by Geoff Holder)*

there was £26 left over when the Dunning gun club was wound up, and so he was employed to cut a hole in the dyke, erect a gate and steps, and fence off the monument. If you look just to the right as you go up the steps you will see Mr Doig's name and the date of the works, scratched out in cement. It was his birthday.

The gate was burned by vandals soon after it was erected and so has not been replaced. On 5 or 6 September 1998 further vandalism smashed the cross. On 19 November Scone stonemasons Billy Traill and Graeme Malcolm repaired the damage free of charge. Some news reports of the time stated the cross had been completely replaced, but T&M Stonemasonry told me they simply reused the original parts, joining them back together. The repair can be seen at the rear of the cross. Further ameliorative repairs took place in 2001, with David Doig repairing the fence with material supplied by farmer David Neil, and mason Stewart Henderson re-cementing the interior core while leaving the exterior appearance untouched. The monument is one mile west of Dunning, on the B8062 (Grid reference NO006140).

A MODERN HORROR

In 1997 Myra Hindley, without doubt Britain's most notorious female murderer, wrote that she knew people would have liked to throw her into a pond three times, 'to discover if I sank or swam'. 'Ducking' a witch was an English practice, not usually a Scottish one, but nonetheless it was a penetrating insight. Child-murder was one of the crimes traditionally associated with malevolent witches; in September 1965, Myra Hindley and her lover Ian Brady left behind the mean streets of Manchester for a jaunt to Scotland, and visited the Maggie Wall monument. By this date the Moors Murderers, as they later came to be known, had already killed four children. Brady knew the area from a childhood holiday in 1949, and the couple took photographs of each other at the monument. One of them shows Hindley on the cairn, the word 'witch' clearly visible behind her. The couple stole a stone from the cairn and took it home for their little garden rockery. A short time later they committed their final murder in Manchester, and were arrested. The details of the visit and the stone-theft are in *One of Your Own: The Life and Death of Myra Hindley* by Carol Ann Lee.

Myra Hindley died in prison in 2002. Ian Brady remains in custody. I elected not to include the photograph here.

FIVE

KATE McNIVEN, THE WITCH OF MONZIE

BURN THE WITCH!

Everyone in the Crieff area knows the story of Kate McNiven. How she was accused of witchcraft by the minister and people of Monzie, dragged to the top of the hill called The Knock and burned, but not before she cursed those responsible for her fate. Unlike Maggie Wall, Kate has no monument, but her name is all over the landscape, with Kate McNiven's Crag, Stone, Gate and Bridge still in existence. With this level of fame it must be a foregone conclusion that she had been a real person, must it not?

'The burning of Kate Neiving on Knock Hill, Crieff' by Robert Rule, 1918. *(Reproduced by kind permission of Perth Museum and Art Gallery, Perth and Kinross Council)*

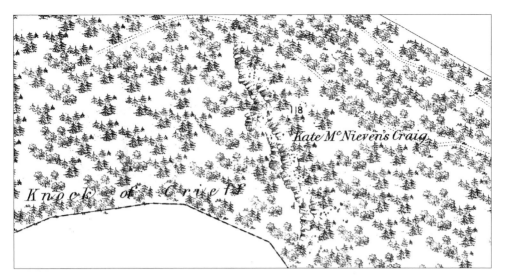

'Kate McNieven's Craig', as shown on the first edition of the Ordnance Survey map in the 1860s. *(Courtesy A.K. Bell Library, Local Studies)*

If only it was that simple. The story of Kate McNiven twists together folklore, fancy, fantasy – and perhaps facts – into a complex tale where nothing is certain. Kate McNiven is as 'real' as Robin Hood, King Arthur or Merlin the Magician; which is to say, we have no idea whether she was real at all. At times, attempting to find the 'truth' about Kate has been like trying to nail jelly to a wall.

THE STANDARD STORY

As with all good legends, the story comes in various forms, but the core details remain the same. Kate was the nursemaid to the young heir of the Inchbrakie family, whose lands were east of Crieff. One day the lad's father, the Laird, went to Dunning to take dinner with the Rollo family at Duncrub Castle. As was usual at the time he carried his cutlery with him, the material culture of the times not extending to families owning spare eating utensils. At one point he found himself distracted by a bee. When his attention returned again to the table, his precious knife and fork were missing. Back at Inchbrakie, the Laird mentioned the puzzling loss to Kate, who immediately located them. By this point the young heir had conceived a dislike for the nurse, and the case of the missing cutlery provided the catalyst: Kate was hunted out of her cottage in Monzie, just north of Crieff, a few miles from Inchbrakie. She was carried up the Knock, tied to a stake and burned alive, the proceedings enthusiastically witnessed by the minister of Monzie, some local gentlemen, and the people of the district. (In some versions she was condemned by the Presbytery of Auchterarder.)

The Laird of Inchbrakie had somehow been kept in the dark about all this, and when he found his old retainer had been taken, he rode to the spot and pleaded for Kate's life. The burning was taking place outside his own lands, and even in a different parish, and so the Laird had no power to enforce his will. He was ignored and the execution proceeded.

If we ignore the ridiculous story of the bee, it is only at this point that the proceedings take a turn to the supernatural. Kate supposedly bent her neck down and bit a blue bead off her necklace, then spat it out at the Laird of Inchbrakie. She prophesised that if his family kept the charm three things would result: the Graemes of Inchbrakie would always have a direct male heir, the family would not lose its property, and, more mysteriously, something would come out of the hill called the King's Craig that would do them all good.

Having demonstrated her gratitude to the one person who tried to save her, Kate then vented her wrath on her persecutors. She prophesised that as long as the Shaggie Burn that runs through Monzie continued on its present course, a three-fold curse would fall on the village – the mirror-image of the prophecy granted to the Inchbrakie family. The estate of the Laird of Monzie, on whose land she was to be murdered, would never pass from father to son; the Kirktown of Monzie and its ministers would never prosper; and the village would always have amongst it inhabitants a drunkard or an idiot. After this, she was consumed by the flames.

The location of the execution varies on who is telling the story – in some versions it occurred on the plain below the Knock; in others she was burned (or strangled) at the very top of the hill, then placed in a barrel of burning tar and rolled down the hill.

Some versions of the story state that Kate's fate was mysteriously linked to a thorn tree in Dunning: when the tree was destroyed in the burning of Dunning by the retreating Jacobite army in 1715, Kate is supposed to have said, 'Alas, the thorn's felled, and I'm undone!' Another detail sometime added is that she had a presentiment that the young heir of Inchbrakie would bring about her doom; she therefore tried to poison him and he found out, thereby setting in course the events that led to her execution.

THE WITCH WHO NEVER WAS?

The basic objections to Kate as a real person are similar to those advanced in the Maggie Wall scenario. There is no trace of her in any official records, plus executing someone for witchcraft without a legal Commission was outright murder, and would attract the unwelcome attention of the Privy Council. If the minister of Monzie had genuinely participated in the unlicensed public execution of a witch, he would have suffered for his actions.

There are other issues with the standard narrative. If the Laird of Inchbrakie was so miffed at his retainer being executed, why did he not complain to the Privy Council and have the perpetrators investigated? Did the credulity of the witchcraft era really extend to the point that people believed a woman could transform into a bee? Why reward the Inchbrakie family when it was the young heir who had shopped her? The 'blue bead' turned out to be a moonstone sapphire – what would a poor woman be doing with such a precious stone in her possession? Sapphires originate from Asia or Australia, so the chances of a poor nursemaid owning such a precious and exotic stone are most unlikely. And if it really was valuable, why had someone not stolen it off her when she was tied up? Can you really bite something off a necklace when your arms are tied to a stake? And then the usual practice in a witchcraft execution was to strangle the convicted person to death, and then burn their body – burning alive was extremely unusual.

So from both a documentation and a practical point of view, we are entitled to ask: did the execution really take place? And was Kate McNiven a real individual?

FRAGMENTS OF HISTORY

Although Kate features in several works of local and more general history, none of them date from earlier than the 1800s, and thus appeared long after the witchcraft trials ceased (the last was in 1722, in Dornoch, Sutherland, although there were very few after 1705). It is notable that none of these books can agree on the date on which she was supposedly executed. Although a few of these written descriptions include a reference to a primary document of the time, the original references themselves are tantalisingly ambiguous. Nowhere is there an undisputed mention of Kate such as a trial transcript, or a memoir, or a mention in the parish records. Many nineteenth-century writers seem to have gleaned their information from hearsay, rumour and folk anecdote – stories that people tell each other round the fire. By the time Kate made it to the printed page, she was already the stuff of legend.

The first mention of Kate McNiven in print is in the 1818 edition of *Memorialls* by the Revd Robert Law – in a footnote the editor, Charles Kirkpatrick Sharpe, makes a brief reference to Catherine Niven at Crieff. Sharpe's later *History of Witchcraft in Scotland* describes an unnamed witch who was strangled and burnt on the Knock of Crieff between 1668 and 1683. In 1845 the *New Statistical Account* for the county of Perth stated she had been executed between 1711 and 1722. The year 1845 also saw the appearance of *The Holocaust; or, the Witch of Monzie* by the Revd George Blair, minister of Monzie in 1843-44, probably the most influential of the locally-published works; Blair gave the date of execution as 1715, even though he could find no reliable record, and much of the work is of his own invention. Sinclair Korner's *Rambles Round Crieff*, published in 1862, repeated the 1715 date. The *New Ordnance Gazetteer of Scotland* (1896) says the execution occurred between 1710 and 1723. *Chronicles of Strathearn* by W.B. Macdougall (also published in 1896) disagrees, noting the date as 1563, this date repeated by Alexander Porteous' 1912 book *The History of Crieff*; *Orr and Sable* by Louisa G. Graeme (1903) gives 1715 to 1720, which is generally agreed with by Robert Scott Fittis, writing in *Romantic Narratives from Scottish History and Tradition* the same year. Finally, George Black in *A Calendar of Cases of Witchcraft in Scotland* (published in 1938) lists the date as 1615, 'but uncertain'.

So we have dates for the supposed execution in 1563, 1615, 1668-1683, 1711-1722, 1710-1723, 1715, and 1715-1720. Several of the descriptions of the events – including the Graeme family's own account – give the name of the young heir of Inchbrakie as Patrick Graeme, whose swarthy complexion gave him the nickname 'Black Pate'. Patrick was a fighting man, distinguishing himself in the service of the Marquis of Montrose during the civil wars of the seventeenth century. Black Pate died around 1687 – so if he was genuinely part of Kate's story all the later dates for the execution are nonsense. On the other hand, Black Pate is the most famous member of the family – perhaps his celebrity was simply 'folded in' to the drama of Kate's capture and murder.

Could other elements of the story provide a clue? The tale of the Laird of Inchbrakie going to dinner in Dunning may mean there was a family connection between the two estates. A good candidate for this is George Graeme of Inchbrakie, who succeeded to the Lairdship in 1555 and died in 1576. He was married to the daughter of Andrew, 6th Lord Rollo, so he could have been visiting his father-in-law. Does this provide a clue, locating the execution in the late sixteenth century, when witch trials were just beginning, rather than the early eighteenth century, by which point they had all but vanished? There again, the fork was unknown in sixteenth-century Britain, but this just may mean new fashions in cutlery were grafted on to the story at a later date.

Another hint to a different period – the seventeenth century – comes from the way Monzie changed hands (remember, Kate prophesised that Monzie would not pass from father to son). In 1613 Monzie had no male heir and the daughter married Patrick Graeme of Inchbrakie, passing the inheritance to that family. This was another Patrick Graeme – the story is made more complicated by the annoying tendency of the Graemes to name their sons alternately George or Patrick, so there could be several 'Georges' or 'Patricks' alive at any one time. In an undated, unaddressed and unpublished handwritten letter kept in the archives of the University of Dundee, Grace Graeme states that one of Kate's prophecies was that 'no George would go over the Seas to return in safety, and that the Georges would spend that the Patricks made.' In 1666 Monzie again ceased to pass from father to son, being sold to Colin Campbell. Either – or both – of these stories could have given rise to a rumour or an invented tradition about a 'curse' preventing the direct lineal heir inheriting the property. Concerns about inheritance dominated the thinking of the landowning classes, and it is easy to see how these events could have generated a preoccupation with a 'curse'.

In the end, though, all this is the most insubstantial of data – wisps of rumour, speculation and possibilities. To dig further into the story of Kate McNiven, we have to look beyond the minutiae of local history. We have to delve into the realm of mythology and supernatural belief.

NICNEVEN – THE QUEEN OF THE WITCHES

In the different versions of the story we find Kate's name spelled variously as Catherine Niven, Kate M'Nieven, Kate McNeiving, Kate Nike Neiving, and other variations. (Note that Nic – 'daughter of' – is the female equivalent of the Gaelic patronymic Mac – 'son of'.) One of the possible sources for the Kate McNiven story is that she is simply the avatar of a bigger character – NicNiven, a powerful witch from Scottish mythology. Or, at least, Scottish fantasy.

NicNiven or NicNeven is a shadowy figure, with just one mention in the literature of post-Reformation Scotland. She first appears out of the mist of history in a poem by Alexander Montgomery entitled *The Flyting of Montgomery and Polwart*. Montgomery was a member of the Scottish élite, and the poem was almost certainly read out in the presence of the young James VI and the Court. It may have been written around 1580. Flytings were the sixteenth century equivalent of modern 'Your Mama…' insult games, a slanging match where two poets took it in turns to be as creatively insulting as possible to each other. The Flyting is very long, with each poet speaking in turn on the page. At one point Montgomery claims his rival Patrick Hume of Polwarth ('Polwart') was the child of a female ape and an elf or a fairy (in the form of an incubus, a sexual demon), and that he was fostered by witches.

After his birth, Polwart is cursed by the three Weird Sisters (not Macbeth's witches, but the more potent beings called the Fates or the Kindly Ones, the trio of intelligences who decide the fate of us all). One curse, given without context, introduces NicNeven for the first time: 'Nicneven… shall nourish thee twyse.' It is not clear why NicNeven needs to breast-feed Polwart twice, but perhaps it simply doubles the insult. Soon after, the Sisters depart and

NicNiven arrives: 'Nicneven with her nymphs, in number nine… venerable virgins, whom the world calls witches.' They ride in on brood sows, black female dogs, stags, or the backs of monks. It is All Hallows Eve, Hallowe'en. NicNiven appears casually, without any build-up, in the same way that a contemporary celebrity needs no introduction when they bound on stage at a pantomime – so we can assume that in 1580 everyone in the audience was familiar with the character. Nicneven and her crew proceed to 'baptise' Polwart in the name of Hecate, the 'goddess of the witches', a name well-known from Classical sources. The hellish cavalcade then depart, and send baby Polwart off in a basket to his foster-mother – 'Kate of Crieff'.

Here we enter what scholar Alison Hanham described in a 1969 essay on NicNiven as 'one of the minor mare's nests of Scottish history.' Is 'Kate of Crieff' our Kate McNiven? If so, the poem makes it clear she is a completely different person to NicNiven, who is seen as a witch-leader, while Kate is simply a wet-nurse who has the misfortune to breastfeed Polwart for seven years, during which time the child neither speaks nor grows. This peevishness is typical of changelings, bad-tempered fairies foisted onto humans, and of course Polwart is the son of an elf. (When the child's screams become too much, both elves and apes appear with food, and everything falls apart into magical chaos, which proves the old actors' adage of not working with children or animals. Or fairies, for that matter).

Alternatively, as rationalising nineteenth-century writers contended, is the phrase 'Kate of Crieff' just a misreading of the Skait (Gaelic, *sgeith*) of Crieff, an ancient place of judgement just south of the town, where the Court of Stewartry met? And is it relevant that 'Kate of Crieff' was a wet-nurse, while the traditional story of Kate McNiven has her as the nursemaid of the heir of Inchbrakie?

Sadly, NicNiven disappears from the printed page for the following two centuries. Her next appearance is in 1808, in J. Jamieson's *Etymological Dictionary of the Scottish Tongue*, which has the definition: 'Nicneven – A name given to the Scottish Hecate or mother-witch, also called the Gyrecarlin.' (In the Flyting, of course, NicNiven and Hecate are shown to be two separate beings.) Two years later R.H. Cromek included a reference in his *Remains of Nithsdale and Galloway Song*:

> The Gyre Carline; who is reckoned the mother of glamour, and near a-kin to Satan himself.
> She is believed to preside over the 'Hallowmass Rades'; and mothers frequently frighten their
> children by threatening to give them to McNeven, or the Gyre Carline. She is described as
> wearing a long gray mantle, and carrying a wand, which, like the miraculous rod of Moses,
> could convert water into rocks and sea into solid land.'

And in 1820 Walter Scott placed her in his novel *The Abbot*: 'For a' that folk said about the skill and witcheries of Mother Nicneven… the auld Popish witchwife [with] eyes of swarthy fire… She was no common spaewife, this Mother Nicneven… She had lords and lairds that would ruffle for her.' Scott's own historical note to the passage reads: 'This was the name given to the grand Mother Witch, the very Hecate of Scottish popular superstition. Her name was bestowed, in one or two instances, upon sorceresses, who were held to resemble her by their superior skill in 'Hell's black grammar.'

Carline is a Scots word for witch or old woman. According to John Ewart Simpkins' *Folk-Lore Concerning Fife with Some Notes on Clackmannan and Kinross-Shires*, Carlin Maggie was

The rock pillar of Carlin Maggie on the Lomond Hills. *(Courtesy Kinross Museum)*

the chief witch in the Lomond Hills above Loch Leven. She got into a rumble with grumpy old Satan, who promptly turned her into a pillar of rock. The fossilised Carlin can still be seen on Bishop Hill – although, compared to the old photograph, she has lost some of her height to recent frost action.

The Gyre Carline appears as a character in several sixteenth-century Scottish poems, where she is regarded as the Queen of the Fairies or Witches. At some point between Montgomery's tirade of creative abuse, and the lexicographer Jamieson compiling his dictionary, the Gyre Carline and NicNiven obviously became identified as the same individual, but we do not know when or how this happened. This conflation of supernatural beings in folktales is quite common. In their book *Scottish Fairy Belief*, historians Lizanne Henderson and Edward Cowan also wonder whether 'NicNiven' is derived from 'Neamhain' (pronounced Neaven), one of the terrifying Irish goddesses of war.

It is possible that NicNiven became to be used not so much a name as a title or nickname – in the same way that aspiring boxers would once be called 'a real Joe Louis', or struggling writers addressed as 'Oy! Shakespeare!' This might explain a few other brief references in the historic record. On 12 July 1643 John McIlvorie was put on trial for witchcraft in Crieff, although there is no record of the outcome – he was probably released. His mother-in-law was Neane MacClerick, a widow who claimed to be the niece of 'NikNeveing'.

We have much more detail on another trial of the same year, which saw fifty-six-year-old Kinross-shire man Johnne Brughe executed at Edinburgh on 24 November. Brughe, known as the 'warlock of Glendevon', was a man of considerable reputation. He could cast fairy darts ('elf shot') into animals and cure cattle with a pair of enchanted stones, as well as offering a wide range of healing for various ailments. On the dark side, he was accused of meeting with Satan and digging up corpses from the graveyards at Glendevon and Muckart and setting the decaying flesh above the doors of byres and stables – an action that would magically harm the animals. Brughe was implicated by the confession of Katherine Mitchell, who had been executed in Culross the previous year.

Brughe's interest for us is that he claimed to have learned his witchcraft from a sixty-year-old widow named Neane Nikclerith, clearly the same woman as John McIvorie's mother-in-law, and that she was the niece of 'Nike Neveing, that notorious infamous witche in Monzie'. This is the first reference linking NicNiven to Monzie.

Is this a solid clue? Possibly not. The original document uses the word 'Monyie'. Monzie is pronounced 'Mon-ee' but there is another placename near Cupar in Fife, pronounced the same but spelt Moonzie. And in 1569 a woman named Niknevin was executed at St Andrews, just a few miles from Moonzie. This was the period when Lord James Stuart, the Earl of Moray, was Regent of Scotland, Mary Queen of Scots having abdicated in favour of her infant son James (later James VI), and the case is mentioned in the earliest biography of the King, *The Historie and Life of King James the Sext*. From Stirling, the Regent 'passed to St. Andrews, where a notable sorceress called Nicniven was condemned to the death and brunt.' More detail appears in a letter written by Sir John Mure of Caldwell from St. Andrews on 10 May 1569:

> Niknevin tholes an assize [stands trial] this Tuesday; it is thought she shall suffer the death; some others believe not. If she dies, it is feared she do cummer [accuse others] and cause many others to incur danger; but as yet for no examination my Lord Regent nor the ministers can make she will confess no witchcraft nor guilt, nor others, but says to my Lord Regent and the examiners that it is nought that has caused her to be taken but the Pottingars [Apothecaries]; and that for envy, by reason she was the help of them that was under infirmity; and speaks the most crafty speaking as is possible to ane woman to be so far past in years who is ane hundred years.

Here we have a hundred-year-old female healer articulately arguing against her accusers (who included not just the Regent but the powerful Calvinist preacher John Knox), refusing to be browbeaten into confessing, and placing the blame for her plight on the professional jealousy of the local (male) apothecaries. Is it possible that this formidable woman's reputation was so great that she had already been granted the honorific title 'NicNiven' by her neighbours? And by her courage and fortitude, did she contribute to the name NicNiven becoming a local legend – which then may have fed into later stories of persecuted women? This was just over a decade before the writing of the Flyting – could the St Andrews NicNiven have already become a byword for witchcraft by 1580? There is not the slightest scrap of evidence for any of this, but I suggest that the claims of Johnne Brughe, John McIlvorie and Neane MacClerick shows that the white-haired old woman from St Andrews became celebrated in legend – and that much of the NicNiven folklore that followed had some of its roots in the brave healer's stance in 1569.

THE PROPHECIES AND THE WITCH'S RING

What of the various prophecies supposedly uttered by Kate at the stake? Revd Blair and other nineteenth-century were adamant that the curses on Monzie had been fulfilled. However, on 28 August 1965 Maitland Makgill Crichton, the Laird of Monzie Castle, wrote to the *Strathearn Herald* pointing out that as he had inherited the title from his father, he was living denial of the curse. Further, the two previous generations had each inherited by direct descent, which rather quashed the idea that 'Monzie would never pass from father to son'.

The Inchbrakie prophecies may be a different story, although as they are positive predictions there is, of course, a strong incentive for people to want them to have come true – particularly if those people are the beneficiaries, i.e. the Graemes. The enigmatic pronouncement about something good coming out of the King's Craig was allegedly fulfilled when the Graemes were so in debt that they were threatened with losing Inchbrakie. The family applied to the Balgowans (known colloquially as the 'Bank of Strathearn') for an additional loan to pay off their creditors, and a servant was despatched to collect the money. The bag of gold was so large he had difficulty getting out of the stable. Upon forcing his way through the door he said the prophecy was now fulfilled, as the lintel above the stable door had been quarried on Kings Craig.

The second prophecy, about the Inchbrakie lands being secure as long as the witch's stone was kept on the ancestral lands, has apparently also come true, although in a negative way. The stone had been set in a gold ring decorated with blue enamel, and was never allowed off the property. Sometime in the 1800s the Laird of Inchbrakie went to India with his regiment, and the house was to be let to strangers. As part of the arrangements, the family's charter chest of papers was sent for safekeeping to Mrs Laurence Graeme, a relative who lived on the outskirts of Crieff, off the Inchbrakie lands. In 1903 Louisa Graeme published a family history, *Orr and Sable, A Book of the Graemes and Grahams*, and she described the events from a personal perspective:

> Her nephew visiting her, opened the box, carrying into the dining-room some papers he wished his aunt to see; amongst them was a small but quaint-looking box or casket. I was present, and with girlish curiosity opened it to find a ring. Never shall I forget my mother's horror and dismay as she turned and saw the precious relic no longer held on the lands of Inchbrakie.

Within a few years part of the estate was sold, with more and more acres lost over the years. Around 1882 or 1885 the entire estate had been sold, and the family moved to England. It was not a disaster, as they prospered very nicely, but it meant the Graemes were no longer 'of Inchbrakie'.

The ring, however, was kept safe, and the third prophecy, that it would ensure each father would have a son to inherit, was closely monitored. Whenever a son of the Graemes married, the ring had been ritually placed on the finger of the bride by her father-in-law, so as to ensure the birth of the son, and hence continue the line of direct heirs. But after the lands were sold, the power waned. Patrick James Frederick Graeme departed to Canada, leaving the ring at a lawyer's office in Edinburgh. He died, unmarried, shortly after the First World War, aged seventy-six – the line was broken.

Only one male member of the family remained, Captain David H. Graeme of the Seaforth Highlanders. He was the nephew of the author of *Orr and Sable*, Louisa Graeme, and the only surviving son of a cousin of P.J.F. Graeme. Captain Graeme married in 1921, and the marriage was blessed with two children – but they were girls. Eight years later, the captain was fifty-four years old and the prospect loomed that there would be no male heir. However, by this date a small portion of the original estate had been recovered, Aberuthven Lodge and its grounds. Captain Graeme had an idea. He visited the lawyer's office in Edinburgh, and obtained the ring. 'There has been no heir born in the direct line since the family sold the Inchbrakie property forty years ago,' he told a newspaper. 'My father's first cousin, who was the last head of the family, died childless. My brother also died childless, and my father is dead. I have two daughters. I thought of the family legend and had faith in it.' He travelled to Aberuthven Lodge: 'I took the stone and buried it under the floor of the house on the only piece of land remaining to the family.' The fertility magic worked: an heir was born in 1929, duly announced in the newspapers of the time (typical headlines included 'A Witch's Prophecy: How It Was Fulfilled'), and reworked by Crieff resident Norah Morrison in the *Strathearn Herald* on 14 September 1965. Successive generations have proved equally adept at producing sons. At the time of writing, Captain Graeme's great-great-grandson by the direct line is enjoying primary school.

Prophecies and legends, however, are difficult things to contain – different versions keep breaking out and manifesting elsewhere. Local man James Sheriff related to me a family story he had been told several times in his younger days at Fowlis Wester, three miles or so east of Monzie. The story was that Kate McNiven had fallen out with the minister at Fowlis Wester and placed a curse on the manse, predicting that no male child would be born there for 200 years. When James came into the world in 1931, it was widely stated by all and sundry that he was the first boy born there for two centuries. The manse had been continually occupied during that time, and the stork had brought many daughters over the years, but no sons. James' mother knew about the curse before he was born. She was married in 1928 and had a daughter a year later, thus fulfilling the usual run of things, so when her son was born it was the talk of the village. According to James, his mother dined out on this story for many years. It sounds so similar to the Graeme story, and the dates are close as well, but I suspect this is an entirely separate, genuine tradition that flourished within Fowlis Wester.

THE FATE OF THE WITCH'S RING

But what of the witch's ring? It is no longer buried beneath Aberuthven Lodge, as that property was sold again in 1971. When I wrote *The Guide to Mysterious Perthshire* a few years ago, I wondered what had become of the ring. I am delighted to say it still exists, and these days is in safekeeping. It has no inscription, and a pair of regular-cut stones flanks the oval blue sapphire. The documented references to the ring only go back to the earlier nineteenth century. Could it have been some kind of charm stone, of the kind other Scottish families used as a healing stone, usually dipped in water? Or was it a stone of some other kind of significance that somehow became associated with the Kate McNiven story, possibly under the Romantic influence of Walter Scott?

Kate McNiven's Ring today. *(Alex Graeme)*

The ring and the 'Witch's Relic'. *(Alex Graeme)*

The ring and the 'relic' in their storage case. *(Alex Graeme)*

Scott Fraser, who was brought up on the neighbouring Abercairney estate in the 1970s, related an entirely separate tradition regarding the ring to me. Kate McNiven was part of daily folklore – if he behaved badly the young boy was told that he would be 'sent to Kate's'. Scott's father worked on the estate and told him his version of the Kate story. She was accused not just of stealing cutlery, but also jewellery – specifically, a silver ring. Protesting her innocence, she prophesised that Inchbrakie Castle would burn to the ground, and when this happened events would prove she was free of guilt. When the house caught fire the body of a mouse was found – with a silver ring round its neck. This ring was what later became known as the 'witch's ring'. According to the *New Statistical Account* of 1845, Inchbrakie Castle may have been burnt by Oliver Cromwell in the seventeenth century. This fascinating variant on the standard story bears little resemblance to the usual published tradition regarding the ring, and only came about through a chance contact. How many other unpublished 'unauthorised versions' of the story could be circulating among the traditions and handed-down family tales of people in the Crieff area?

The ring is currently stored alongside a curious item called the 'witch's relic'. As the image shows, this consists of the representation of a human skull linked to a heart-shaped item bearing the words 'Cruell Death'. This is turn is suspended from a chain of some seventy links. The skull has gold-painted 'hair' and splashes of deep blue colouring in its eye-sockets, nose and teeth, and on the forehead. The heart is the same dark blue colour and has two tiny gold 'wings' that are the projecting points of crossed bones.

This enigmatic pendant appears for the first time in print in 1903, when a photograph was featured in *Orr and Sable*, but without any description. Louisa Graeme's book is so thoroughly detailed that the absence of any information on this item may be telling. Was it a trinket that was picked up at a later date and placed with the witch's ring just because it was 'spooky'? The phrase 'Cruell Death' occurs in the works of any number of English poets, for example: 'For still I live in spight of cruell death' (Thomas Watson, *The Tears of Fancie,* 1593) and, 'Cruell death vanquishing so noble beautie' (Edmund Spenser, *The Visions Of Petrarch*, 1591). In fact, its typical usage falls within the Elizabethan period (1558-1603). *Brewer's Dictionary of Phrase and Fable* notes that during the time of Elizabeth I, prostitutes and brothel-keepers used to wear a ring in the form of a death's head. Is this a meaningful link, or is it just coincidence? Could this mean that the 'relic', or part of it, genuinely dates from the late sixteenth century? Or is it some kind of faux eighteenth-century piece, a fake made for an antiquarian collector? Why, when the ring is mentioned several times, is the relic absent from family traditions? As is by now standard practice for the Kate McNiven story, the more we think we know, the more it becomes clear we know almost nothing.

KATE MCNIVEN IN THE LANDSCAPE

If you want to go looking for Kate in the landscape, there are several places to visit. Inchbrakie is now a private estate and there is nothing relevant to see anyway, but her name lingers elsewhere.

Kate McNieven's Craig (National Grid Reference NN878 238)
The most obvious location is The Knock, 911ft/278m high and a popular excursion from Crieff. Kate McNieven's Craig (this is the spelling preferred by the Ordnance Survey) is at

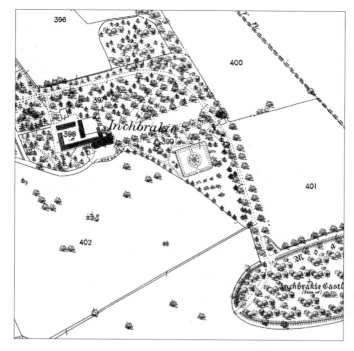

The site of Inchbrakie Castle, and its replacement house, on the Ordnance Survey first edition map. *(Courtesy A.K. Bell Library, Local Studies)*

the northeastern end of the hill. According to J.B. Paterson, writing in the *Strathearn Herald* on 7 August 1965, the burning spot was a little east of the now-lost Wishing Tree, which once stood isolated on the plateau with a view over Monzie Castle. A long-term resident of Crieff informed me that as a young man he had been told by a neighbour in his sixties that the spot where Kate had been burned could be easily recognised – because nothing would grow there.

Kate McNiven's Stone aka The Witch's Stone (NN8798 2429)

This is a prehistoric standing stone visible from the track that runs through the private Monzie estate. Ask permission at the gatehouse on the west side of the Gilmerton to Monzie minor road, then walk 800m up the track. According to one version of the legend, Kate was placed in a barrel of tar which was set alight and rolled down the Knock, coming to rest here. Alternatively, this is where she was burned. I wouldn't place any money on either story being in any way true. On its way to the Witch's Stone, the track passes a stone circle (NN88162417) with an excellent cupmarked stone. There is no folklore linking Kate to this circle. The route gives excellent views of Kate McNieven's Craig. Please do not climb barbed wire fences or damage crops.

Kate McNiven's Bridge (NN8785 2505)

The minor road that runs through the hamlet of Monzie crosses the Shaggie Burn, the stream that features in one of Kate's prophecies. Immediately east of the present bridge is the single arch of the original stone bridge, which can be impossible to see behind the trees in summer. This was sometimes called the Witch's Bridge or Kate McNiven's Bridge. Scott Fraser, who has already been mentioned, recalled that in the 1970s his family would visit the bridge on Easter Sunday or Monday, and roll hard-boiled eggs down the incline while reciting a rhyme about Kate being rolled down The Knock.

Kate McNiven's Stone (a prehistoric standing stone) with Kate McNiven's Craig behind. *(Photo by Geoff Holder)*

Another view of the Craig and The Knock, this time from the cupmarked stone in Monzie stone circle. *(Photo by Geoff Holder)*

Above: Kate McNiven's Gate at Monzie. Note the waterworn stones above the gateway. Kate McNiven's Bridge is hidden in the trees to the right of the present bridge. *(Photo by Geoff Holder)*

Left: The Shaggie Burn at Kate McNiven's Bridge. The stream features in one of her prophecies. *(Photo by Geoff Holder)*

Kate McNiven's Gate (NN87838 24998)

Immediately south of the road bridge in Monzie is a curious gateway. *The Holocaust*, the influential book on Kate McNiven written by the Revd George Blair of Monzie in 1845, describes it as 'Kate M'Niven's gate' and 'M'Niven's antique doorway.' *Orr and Sable*, published in 1903, quotes an unnamed Crieff resident's description of it as, 'The very ancient gateway that spans the Shaggie at Monzie village, and which leads to the Manse and to the Green, has been known since the days of the witch as 'Kate M'Niven's Yett'; she passed through it on her way to the Craig.' The same book has a note from James Taylor of Gilmerton: 'There used to be a stone on the top of the Gate through which poor Kate was hunted to her doom, which stone has been always called 'Kate M'Niven.'

The gateway is topped with two riverbed stones sculpted into interesting shapes by the stream; elsewhere in Perthshire there are numerous examples of such water-worn stones placed at gateways, entrances and bridges. They have an apotropaic function, that is, they guard against the entry or passage of evil. It is hard to tell the age of the gateway, but it has a late eighteenth-century/early nineteenth-century look. Perhaps its Romantic appearance brought it into the orbit of the witch legend? Or it was constructed as part of the witch legend? Scott Fraser remembers being told it originally stood at Kate's cottage, which was supposedly southeast of Monzie, close to The Knock, although it seems too fancy an adornment for a poor nursemaid's cottage. His father James Wannan, who was born in 1930, told Scott that if you passed through the gate 'thinking bad thoughts', bad things would happen to you.

Orr and Sable mentions Kate McNiven's Well, as well as Kate McNiven's Cave. I have been unable to locate either.

KATE IN LITERATURE AND ART

As well as her appearance in Blair's imaginative narrative poem in *The Holocaust*, Kate was eulogised ('Behold in me, as sure's ye're livin' / The ghost o' pair auld Kate McNiven') by Duncan MacTavish in his 1897 work *The Witch of Monzie*:

> At ither times, upon the mair,
> I wis seen tae hirple like a hare,
> Decoyin' folk amang the bogs;
> till they were drooned amang the frogs;
> Then, on a broomstick, I wid ride
> Swift as a racehorse in its pride;
> Tirlin' beeskeps an' witchin' kye
> Till they frae giein' milk gaed dry;

In 1832 James Stewart's play *The Witch of Monzie* was produced in Crieff, with the added attraction of the witch being burned on stage. There was no information on whether there were any problems in supplying enough replacement leading ladies.

Robert Rule (1892-1964) painted 'The burning of Kate Neiving' in 1918. For a number of years the watercolour was on display in Crieff Town House. The original is now in storage but a small black and white reproduction can be seen at the Perth Museum and Art Gallery.

THE EVIL BEE

Kate was a regular feature in the *Strathearn Herald* in 1965, with believers and sceptics laying into each other. The correspondence came to a close with a letter from a reader named Black who had been reading the articles and was attacked by an unnaturally persistent wasp or bee: 'I began to be a little frightened now. Could this be a modern manifestation of the famous witch herself, angrily protesting against my scepticism? Perhaps some other of your readers may have had similar strange experiences.'

THE WITCH THAT WAS?

Can anything be said for certain about the reality of Kate McNiven's existence? The short answer is: no. There is no documentary evidence for her life or death. The ring – although miraculously still preserved – has no solid provenance and could have been grafted on to the existing tale. The landscape legends are just that – legends. We are therefore left with a number of possibilities:

1. Kate McNiven did not exist. Despite the breadth and depth of local tradition, she is a story, nothing more. The story may have been created in the early nineteenth century when Walter Scott's influence was at its height, and his *Letters on Demonology and Witchcraft* (published in 1830) persuaded many a noble family to generate Romantic narratives of spooks and curses.

2. Kate McNiven is a stand-in for many other poor women who were judicially murdered for the supposed crime of witchcraft. She is a composite figure, eliding all the complex details of legal issues, trial machinations, dates and names, and instead presenting a simple, straightforward fireside tale that evokes sympathy and presents a simple moral: injustice is punished by a curse, and kindness is rewarded by a boon.

3. Kate McNiven is a localised retelling of the case of Niknevin, burned in 1569 at St Andrews. That old woman may have come from Moonzie in Fife, and the similarity of the placenames has caused the tale to be transferred to Monzie in Perthshire.

4. Kate McNiven did exist somewhere, but she was not executed at Monzie, and her name is a nickname or honorific derived from the folklore surrounding the mythological witch-leader NicNiven.

5. Kate McNiven's story is a confused retelling of a genuine local case. In 1683–4 the ten-year-old daughter of Monzie farmer Donald McGrigor was extensively troubled by fits and visions, in which she was visited by the Devil and two female witches. After being apparently cured by prayer and a divine intervention by a pair of pure white hands, she held regular conversations with angels. The case became something of a dispute between the various religious factions that were in conflict in Scotland at the time, each seeking confirmation of their beliefs in the opinions of the angels. The case is extensively described in the Revd Robert Law's book *Memorialls*. On the face of it, it seems unlikely that this extraordinary case could have become so distorted as to be transmuted into the familiar details of Kate's life and death, but stranger things have happened in folklore (for example the brutal Crusader and absent king, Richard I, becomes the saviour of the *Robin Hood* tales or a wild man from the Scottish Borders is mythologised as the suave kingmaker Merlin).

6. Kate McNiven was real, but the details of her case have been obscured, lost, or unrecorded. This last possibility allows me a moment of wild speculation, unsupported by any evidence. We know that witchtrials in Scotland were legalistic affairs, and that severe penalties awaited those who murdered witches outside the legal framework. We know that witchcraft became a capital crime when it was passed into law on 4 June 1563 – the triumphant Protestant ideologues of the recently-successful Reformation pushed it through as part of their beliefs. There is an entry in the *Source-book of Scottish Witchcraft* that a woman called Nik Neving was executed in 1563 at Monaie – she was 'mentioned as a witch by an accused person'. The *Source book*, a compendium of cases from various sources, has been superseded by the *Survey of Scottish Witchcraft*, which regards the entry as unreliable, and does not feature it. We know 'NicNiven' was a well-kent name by 1580, and that a woman named 'Kate of Crieff' was described in a poem as being a nursemaid with a relationship to the supernatural. For all these reasons I reject any possibility that Kate McNiven was executed after 1600.

But what if Kate McNiven belonged to a period just around the passing of the Witchcraft Act of 1563? The actual details of the new law would be unfamiliar to the vast majority of people, and it might take some time for the procedure to percolate through to rural districts. If Kate was tried and executed at the cusp of the new world of witchcraft law, perhaps it was all a bit *ad hoc* – with her persecutors making it up as they went along. With no guidelines, the minister and the local gentry could have acted through ignorance of the law, and not held a proper trial, or even recorded the episode. Perhaps Kate simply slipped through the cracks, an event that could not have been possible once the law became established and procedures were laid down. The horrific episode lingered in local memory and then local folklore, gaining new additions and embellishments down the centuries. The witch may not even have been called Kate McNiven, the name being one of the accretions gathered over time.

So was Kate McNiven executed sometime around 1560 to 1563, and her fate not recorded? Is this why she is still remembered? I have no idea. In the end the only verdict on the case of Kate McNiven is: Not Proven.

SIX

PERSONAL ENCOUNTERS WITH THE PARANORMAL

I saw a host of spectres gaunt,
Striding triumphant o'er the land

William Anderson, *Rhymes, Reveries, and Reminiscences*

In 2010 I placed articles in several Perthshire publications, appealing for readers to contact me with their personal experiences of the paranormal. A number of people got in touch, and what follows are their own stories of visible and invisible entities both benevolent and malevolent, psychic episodes, and strange and marvellous interactions with the natural world and the landscapes around us. As they are largely one-off, spontaneous encounters, I have not been able to investigate them further, and so I present them as they were told to me. I am grateful to all the individuals concerned for permission to use their stories.

DARK FORCES AND ANGELIC ASSISTANCE

For reasons that will quickly become apparent, I have disguised all the names in the following case. Tracy is in her thirties, with a good quality of life, a husband, daughter, job, and a nice home. But it was not always so. When she was growing up she and her two sisters had been systematically sexually abused by their father. Tracy was the youngest, and did not directly learn about the abuse until it happened to her. In retrospect, she believes the horrors of home life somehow called up dark forces. When she was four or five years old she woke up very quickly to see what she described as 'a whirlwind' collapse into the floor at the foot of her bed. Out of this came a figure with a pure white face twisted with hatred, black eyes with no pupils, and wearing a black cloak. Tracy described it as having a definite 'air of evil'. Her sister was in the next bed so she got up and said there was a 'bad man' in the room. Her sister grumpily told her to go to sleep, so Tracy scuttled back into bed without looking at the figure, and hid under the covers. Around about the same age Tracy also had a consistent fear of someone standing at the top of the stairs. These episodes can easily be dismissed as standard childish nightmares and anxieties, somehow reflecting the underlying tensions in the household. However, in adult life the three sisters were discussing their childhoods and they found that each one of them had been genuinely convinced there was a 'darkness' about the house and that something nasty lurked at the top of the stairs. None of them had previously shared this belief with the others.

Although Tracy's mother did not know about the abuse, the marriage fell apart anyway, and Tracy relocated to her new home in a Letham housing estate while her older sisters, April and Stephanie, remained with their father in the North Muirton area of Perth. Some time later their father moved out, and then April went to live with her boyfriend, leaving Stephanie alone in the three-bedroom council house. Steph began to think the house was haunted. The phone would ring with no one at the other end of the line. Strange knocks were heard at the windows. The seventeen-year-old became so terrified she eventually just abandoned the house, leaving it empty. Some time later a woman called at her new address. She nervously explained that she was now the tenant of Steph's old house – and that it was haunted. There was a sense of presence, and of great sadness. Her three young daughters said they 'saw things'. But the tipping point came when had come home one day to find the two-year-old had arranged letters on the wall to spell out the words April, Stephanie and Tracy, the names of the three former occupants. Steph did what she could to reassure the woman, who told her she was going to ask a priest to exorcize the house. Some time later Steph met the woman at the shops, and was told everything had been fine since the blessing.

This occurred around 1990 or 1991. During roughly the same period Tracy was wrestling with her own demons – literally. She was sixteen and in a fragile state emotionally when she got a job in a local chip shop. The two Asian brothers who worked there were kind to her and almost 'adopted' her into their family, often letting her stay over at their flat off Crieff Road. Typically, they would get up early for work while she would sleep late and then potter round the flat, attempting to clear up some of the bachelor mess. She always had an eerie feeling in the flat, a sense of something malevolent watching her as she moved through the rooms. One day she woke about 1 pm with a 'force' on top of her. Although invisible, it felt to her like an old man weighing around fifteen stone. A struggle ensued with the entity attempting to choke her while Tracy tried to push it off her. Eventually she succeeded in getting away, and immediately grabbed her clothes, ran out of the flat, leaving the door open, and jumped on first bus that came along – just to get as far away from the flat as possible. She phoned the brothers, angrily shouting that she was never coming back and didn't want anything to do with them. Not surprisingly, they were confused by her aggressive *volte-face* but she adamantly refused to renew the friendship, and later heard they had moved away.

Shortly before this encounter, Tracy had an experience that literally changed her life. At this point she was probably fifteen, and living with her mum and her mother's new boyfriend. The man was physically abusing her, while the sexual abuse was continuing when she returned to visit her father. She was being bullied at school, and had started delinquent behaviour such as stealing money from her mother's purse. Things were so bad that she decided to commit suicide. Having rejected hanging, drowning and jumping from a great height, Tracy opted for a peaceful death. She went to several chemists and accumulated around a hundred Paracetemol tablets, and set the day and time firmly in her mind. When the date arrived, she waited until everyone had gone out, arranged the pills and a glass of water in the bathroom. She said a short prayer: 'Sorry God, I know it's a sin, I hope I go to Heaven and not to Hell, but I can't carry on.'

As she reached for the pills, she heard a voice calling her name repeatedly. She then became aware of 'an aura of rainbow colours, like a whirlwind, a rainbow whirlwind aura.' Her long hair was streaming in the wind, and she heard voices say 'Tracy, Tracy, one day you will be happy.' Over it all was the impression of invisible wings. The entire experience lasted perhaps ten to fifteen seconds, and at the end of it the troubled teenager knew she had received a divine intervention. All thoughts of suicide were pushed aside. Although it was a long road, her life did improve. Her mother's boyfriend left, her abusive father went to prison for the abuse, she got an education and a job, and met a good man. In Tracy's opinion, angels had visited her that day in the bathroom.

THE 'GHOST' OF SCONE AERODROME

Bankfoot man Thomas Brown joined the Scottish Aero Club in 1980, and subsequently spent many hours at Scone Aerodrome. The new clubroom was opened by Squadron Leader Alfred Smith, who had learned to fly at Scone before the Second World War and qualified as a private pilot at Scone after he left the RAF. During his opening address the distinguished airman mentioned that the aerodrome was known to be haunted, although he gave no details. Some time later Thomas and his wife were relaxing in the clubroom, looking onto the airfield bathed in bright moonlight. It was 10 p.m. on a Sunday night in January 1982 or 1983. Through the window the couple clearly saw a man wearing 'a kind of light boiler suit' walk at a steady pace across the runway in the direction of the hangar. The figure appeared solid and normal in all respects, and was in sight for perhaps thirty seconds. As the airfield was a restricted area the security guard was called. He arrived in less than a minute with his jeep and Alsatian dog and, in company with the witnesses, searched the area with full beams on. Nothing was found. Although it could have been a would-be thief, the guard had responded so quickly that Thomas was convinced no human intruder could have got away.

GENTLE GHOSTS

Many published reports of hauntings are very spectacular, with accounts of apparitions, objects being moved, and similar dramatic events. But one of my correspondents, whom we'll call Sara, is convinced that the majority of hauntings are more subtle, and that most people who experience them in their homes simply deal with them in their own way. Because the incidents are low-key, they are rarely reported, and do not come to the attention of paranormal groups.

Sara's conclusions are based on her conversations with her social circle of spiritualists and clairvoyants, and also on her own experiences. The office worker lives in a historic building in Kinross. Once she had moved in she became aware of a presence within the flat. There was nothing obvious, just footsteps in different rooms, and the kind of low-key sounds you get when someone else is in your house. There was no attempt at communication, and no objects were moved. Sara described it as like having an invisible flatmate. Gillian, a clairvoyant friend, told Sara she had opened up a channel to the spirit, who was an orphan named Cynthia. According to Gillian, Cynthia liked Sara's new puppy and asked that she also get a bird in a cage to keep her company. Sara refused to do this but did agree to Cynthia's request for flowers, so silk flowers are now always on display. Cynthia settled down after a few months and is now less obvious in her sounds, but she still turns up in the dining room. In a work context, Sara's employers once occupied a temporary office at the corner of Scott Street and South Street in the centre of Perth. Two girls on the team persistently claimed there was 'someone there' in the building, but where always laughed down by the team leader. One day all the others were out at lunch break and the normally frantic office was quiet. Sara picked up an abnormally cold sensation and a sense of presence, as if something was trying to 'come through'. She had the feeling that the female energy wished to say she did not mean anyone any harm, and was glad the place was busy – but simply wanted someone to notice her. Once Sara acknowledged the presence, the subtle 'haunting' stopped.

THE SPIRITS OF FOWLIS WESTER

The tiny village of Fowlis Wester is at the centre of a landscape filled with ancient remains – stone circles, cairns and carved stones. West of the hamlet, between Thorn and Crofthead, is a spectacular grouping of standing stones, one pair upright and, further down the slope, another two recumbent (and very large). The National Grid Reference is NN921239.

In June 1998 Scott Fraser's friend, whom we'll call Steve, invited Scott to a party. Scott did not fancy the shindig but as it was the Summer Solstice and a full moon to boot, the two thirty-year-olds decided to walk out to the Fowlis Wester stones. Both men had an interest in esoteric subjects such as earth mysteries, and so this was not an unusual action for them. Scott lived on the Abercairney estate and had often visited the stones with his father.

It took perhaps an hour to reach their destination, the clear evening providing excellent visibility. When they were about 100 yards from the upright stones, both men saw a group of about a dozen adults and children, all wearing dark brown clothes in the style of monks' habits. When the group became aware of Scott and Steve, they stood up and moved to the stones – where they disappeared. Steve was quite scared, and not willing to get closer, but Scott went up and called out, asking them to remain. When he reached the stones he said he 'got the feeling you have when walking along and sensing someone behind you.' The whole encounter had lasted perhaps 30 seconds, and there had been no sound.

In Scott's opinion the stones were a gateway for a spiritual transportation system, and the 'spirit people' had manifested their energy at the stones – when they were disturbed, they put their energy back through the gateway. He called the process 'going to ground'.

As a coda, after Scott's father James Wannan died aged seventy-eight in 2008, Scott went to the stones to think about his father. From his seated position he saw a shape from the corner of his eye, which appeared to be the shadow of a man about 6 or 7ft away. In its shape or outline, Scott recognised the form of his father. The experience gave him great peace of mind.

PIGS FROM THE FUTURE

One of the most commonly reported experiences of extra-sensory perception (ESP) is precognition, that is, a glimpse into the future. In 2005 or 2006 David Cowan was travelling west along the along the 'low road' from Crieff to Comrie. This is the minor road that runs south of the River Earn, and is a pleasant drive through sparsely-populated fields and woodland. As he was motoring happily along, David had a repeating vision of a deer jumping out of the

The two large standing stones at Fowlis Wester, scene of a sighting of 'spiritual beings'. *(Photo by Geoff Holder)*

A group of recumbent standing stones at Fowlis Wester, a hundred yards from the upright stones. *(Photo by Geoff Holder)*

New Strowan Bridge near
Crieff, where David Cowan's
precognitive visions came
true – twice. *(Photo by Geoff
Holder)*

wood and across the road in front of him. The vision was so clear, and repeated so many times, that he had to slow down. The scene was superimposed on his normal visual perception, but exaggerated as if in a dream. After a few minutes he turned right into the minor road that joins the 'high' and 'low' roads and passes the Sir David's Baird Monument. Less than 100 yards before arriving at the New Strowan Bridge, a deer leapt out in front of him. It moved exactly as he had seen it in the recurring vision.

At the time David dismissed it as coincidence – the incident took place just before dusk, which is exactly the time you would expect to see deer. Then about a year later he was taking the same road, again travelling from east to west in the same direction, when he had a repeating vision of a pig with spiky orange hair. His instant reaction was that it was ridiculous nonsense, but then he turned north onto the linking road as before – and in exactly the same place where the deer had jumped out, he came across about ten pigs in a field next to the road. They were feeding from a trough. And they had spiky orange hair. (These may have been Tamworth pigs, a breed noted for their orange coat.)

The pig vision had occurred in broad daylight, not dusk, and at a different time of the year to the deer incident. As with the first precognitive experience, the colours in the vision had a magnified dreamlike quality when compared with the reality. David is well-known in the Crieff area for his interest in lines of earth energy, dowsing and standing stones. In his opinion the key factor in his precognitive visions is that area by the New Strowan Bridge lies on the Highland Boundary Fault. There is an increasing body of evidence that underground geological faulting can somehow influence both the immediate physical environment in strange ways, and also have a profound if little-understood impact on the human brain.

INTERACTIONS WITH THE NATURAL WORLD

The red-berried rowan tree plays a major part in Scottish folklore, its presence is said to magically protect against witches, fairies and evil spirits. In the Highlands and Islands, many deserted or 'cleared' settlements are now little more than a rickle of stones, but the positions of the houses can still be identified by their rowan trees. It was also thought to be bad luck to damage or cut down a rowan. Elma Wood, an eighty-year-old resident of Highland Perthshire, has a thoroughgoing belief in the efficacy of the rowan. Her tenant farmer father told her many tales of rowan folklore. A farmer who tried to cut down a rowan accidentally drove the axe into his leg, and the wound never healed. A farm manager at Clunie near Blairgowrie insisted that an old rowan needed to be felled, else it would damage a fence – the farm forester, however, absolutely refused to do it, saying he would rather lose his job than cut down a rowan. This was not in the distant past, but in the 1970s, and the forester was probably about forty years old.

Elma had always wanted a rowan tree and one day was out for a walk when she found a seedling, so planted it by her gate. Elma's husband David uprooted the rowan and threw it away. A short time later he fell off the roof. When she got another seedling, he chucked it again, and soon suffered a minor stroke. The third time a rowan was planted by Elma and removed by David, David became seriously ill. Within two days he was in hospital, but was sent home because nothing could be found. On the fourth day Elma was convinced David was going to die, and when their GP came to the house he was both shocked at David's condition, and baffled at the cause. A week into the illness David was lying in bed, and during a talk with Elma agreed that she could have a rowan in the garden. The next morning he was completely healed.

The rowan incident occurred in 2002. The following year David developed severe arthritis, and in his last days could not move. In life he had been interested in little more than his job (plumbing) and his fishing, but now his only pleasure was watching the large number of tits, finches, sparrows and other birds that congregated in the garden. He spent all his money on bird food and became deeply attached to the little creatures, which gathered in flocks of sixty or more. David Wood died at 6 a.m. on an October day in 2003. That morning no birds appeared. They did not return for two weeks.

BIBLIOGRAPHY

Anon *Ancient Scottish Superstitions* (Kinross-shire Historical Society; Kinross, n.d.)

Beath, David *The Bishopshire and its People* (David Brown and the Author; Kinross, 1902)

Black, George F. *A Calendar of Cases of Witchcraft in Scotland 1510-1727* (New York Public Library; New York, 1938)

Burns-Begg, Robert 'Notice of Trials for Witchcraft at Crook of Devon, Kinross-Shire, in 1662' in *Proceedings of the Society of Antiquaries of Scotland, Vol 22* (1888)

———— *Witches in Kinross-shire* (The Author; Kinross, 1889)

Campbell, John L. & Trevor H. Hall *Strange Things - The Enquiry by the Society for Psychical Research into Second Sight in the Scottish Highlands, the story of Ada Goodrich Freer, the Ballechin House ghost hunt, and the stories and folklore collected by Fr. Allan McDonald of Eriskay* (Routledge & Kegan Paul; London, 1968)

Clarke, David *The UFO Files: The Inside Story of Real-Life Sightings* (The National Archives; Richmond, 2009)

Cromek, R.H. (ed) *Remains of Nithsdale and Galloway Song* (T. Cadell & W. Davies; London, 1810)

Fife, Malcolm *Scottish Aerodromes of the First World War* (Tempus; Stroud, 2007)

Fittis, Robert Scott *Romantic Narratives from Scottish History and Tradition* (Alexander Gardner; Paisley, 1903)

Fort, Charles *New Lands* (John Brown Publishing; London, 1996)

Fraser, Mark (ed.) *Big Cats in Britain Yearbook 2006* (CFZ Press; Bideford, 2006)

———— *Big Cats in Britain Yearbook 2007* (CFZ Press; Bideford, 2007)

Gage, Mary E. and James E. Gage *The Art of Splitting Stone, early rock quarry methods in pre-industrial New England, 1630-1825* (Powwow River Books; Amesbury, Massachusetts, 2005)

Goodrich-Freer, A. (Miss X) and John, Marquess of Bute *The Alleged Haunting Of B---- House* (George Redway; London, 1899)

Graeme, Louisa G. *Orr and Sable A Book of the Graemes and Grahams* (William Brown; Edinburgh, 1903)

Hall, Trevor *The Strange Case of Ada Goodrich Freer* (Duckworth; London, 1980)

Hamill, Brendan J. 'A Triple Complex of Low-Angle Oblique Impact Structures in the Midland Valley of Scotland' and 'The Loch Leven Crater: Anatomy of a Low-Angle Oblique Impact Structure', Third International Conference on Large Meteorite Impacts, August 2003, Nördlingen, Germany, abstracts nos. 4027 & 4041

Hanham, Alison "The Scottish Hecate': A Wild Witch Chase' in *Scottish Studies* Volume 13, 1969

Harris, John *Inferences from Haunted Houses and Haunted Men* (1901 - online at www.gutenberg.org)

Henderson, Lizanne & Edward J. Cowan *Scottish Fairy Belief: A History,* (Tuckwell Press; East Linton, 2001)

'Historicus' [Thomas M. Tod] *Historic Scenes Within Our Limits – A Midland Scottish Area* (The Kinross-shire Advertiser; Kinross, 1934)

Lee, Carol Ann *One of Your Own: The Life and Death of Myra Hindley* (Mainstream Publishing; Edinburgh, 2010)

Korner, Sinclair *Rambles Round Crieff and Excursions into The Highlands* (no publisher; 1862)

Journal of the Society for Psychical Research, Volume 8 (1897-1898)

Larner, Christina, Christopher Hyde Lee & Hugh V McLachlan *A Source-book of Scottish Witchcraft* (The Grimsay Press; Glasgow, 2005)

Law, Robert (ed. by Charles Kirkpatrick Sharpe) *Memorialls; or, the Memorable Things that fell out within this Island of Brittain from 1638 to 1684* (Archibald Constable and Co.; Edinburgh, 1818)

Linton, E. Lynn *Witch Stories* (Chapman and Hall; London, 1861)

MacCulloch, J. A. 'The Mingling of Fairy and Witch Beliefs in Sixteenth and Seventeenth Century Scotland' in *Folklore,* Vol. 32, No. 4 (1921)

MacDonald, Stuart *The Witches of Fife: Witch-hunting in a Scottish Shire, 1560-1710* (Tuckwell Press; East Linton, 2002)

Macdougall, W.B. *Chronicles of Strathearn* (David Philips; Crieff, 1896)

MacGregor-Comrie, Gordon A. *The Origins and Genealogy of the Landed Families of Strathearn* (MacGregor Publications; Mains of Kirkbuddo, Forfar, 1996)

MacTavish, Duncan *The Witch of Monzie and Other Poems* (H. K. Brown; Crieff, 1897)

Maidment, James (ed.) *Analecta Scotica: Collections Illustrative of the Civil, Ecclesiastical, and Literary History of Scotland* (Thomas G. Stevenson; Edinburgh, 1834)

Minter, Rick 'Big Cats in our outdoors: Just a few escapes or a breeding population?' in *International Urban Ecology Review,* No. 4, 'Exotic and Invasive Plants and Animals' Issue (2009)

Munro, David M. *The Wells of Kinross-shire* (Kinross-shire Historical Society; Kinross, n.d.)

The New Statistical Account of Scotland Vol X Perth (William Blackwood; Edinburgh and London, 1845)

Oldroyd, Granville 'Dangerous Rumours: First World War Scares in Britain' in Watson, Nigel (ed) *The Scareship Mystery: A Survey of Worldwide Phantom Airship Scares (1909-1918)* (Domra Publications; Corby, 2000)

Sharpe, Charles Kirkpatrick *A Historical account of the belief in Witchcraft in Scotland* (Hamilton, Adams; London / Thomas D Morison; Glasgow, 1884)

Shuker, Karl P.N. 'British Mystery Cats – The Bodies of Evidence' in Steve Moore (ed.) *Fortean Studies Volume 2* (John Brown Publishing; London, 1995)

Simpkins, John Ewart (ed.) *Examples of Printed Folk-Lore Concerning Fife with Some Notes on Clackmannan and Kinross-Shires* (Sidgwick & Jackson/The Folklore Society, London, 1914)

Simpson, Jacqueline 'The Weird Sisters Wandering': Burlesque Witchery in Montgomerie's 'Flyting' in *Folklore,* Vol. 106 (1995)

Walker, N.H. *A Historical Stroll Round Fossoway, 1999* (Kinross-shire Historical Society; Kinross, n.d.)

Wilson, John *Dunning: Its Parochial History* (The Constitutional Office; Perth, 1873)

Winyard, Tom *Haunted Houses in Kinross-shire* (Kinross-shire Historical Society; Kinross, n.d.)

Young, David R. *Cleish Castle Historic Notes: A talk given to the Kinross-shire Antiquarian Society on 25 November 1974* (Kinross-shire Historical Society; Kinross, n.d.)

NEWSPAPERS AND MAGAZINES

Blairgowrie Advertiser 15 July 1871

Courier (Dundee) 27 January 2000; 3 February 2000; 2 September 2008; 10 October 2009; 14 June 2010

Daily Express 16 September 2005

Daily Mail 19 September 1996; 5 February 2010

Daily Record 24 February 2003; 25 October 2008

The Dunningite / The Newsletter of the Dunning Parish Historical Society No.14 (January 1996); No.26 (January 1999); No.34 (January 2001)

Evening News (Edinburgh) 30 March 2010

The Herald 28 December 2000

Perthshire Advertiser 29 December 1973; 9 October 2009

Scotland on Sunday 22 March 2009

Strathearn Herald 4 September 1965; 14 September 1965; 22 August 1997; 9 October 9 2009; 16 October 2009; 6 November 2009; 17 September 2010

The Sun 16 September 2005

Sunday Mail 20 April 2003

Sunday Post 15 August 1976

Sunday Telegraph 22 March 2009

Sunday Times 22 March 2009

The Times 8, 10, 12, 21, 22, and 23 June 1897; 16 September 2005

WEBSITES

Big Cats in Britain, www.bigcatsinbritain.org

The Survey of Scottish Witchcraft, www.shc.ed.ac.uk/Research/witches

UK-UFO. www.uk-ufo.co.uk

UNPUBLISHED DOCUMENTS

Papers of the Rollo family of Duncrub, Perthshire at the National Archives of Scotland, Reference GD56

Papers relating to the Witch of Monzie, at Dundee University Archives, Reference GB 0254 MS 135

INDEX